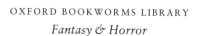

OXFORD BOOKWORMS LIBRARY
Fantasy & Horror

Ghost Stories

Stage 5 (1800 headwords)

Series Editor: Jennifer Bassett
Founder Editor: Tricia Hedge
Activities Editors: Jennifer Bassett and Alison Baxter

RETOLD BY ROSEMARY BORDER

Ghost Stories

OXFORD UNIVERSITY PRESS

Oxford University Press,
Great Clarendon Street, Oxford OX2 6DP

Oxford New York
Auckland Bangkok Buenos Aires Cape Town Chennai
Dar es Salaam Delhi Hong Kong Istanbul Karachi Kolkata
Kuala Lumpur Madrid Melbourne Mexico City Mumbai Nairobi
São Paulo Shanghai Singapore Taipei Tokyo Toronto
with an associated company in Berlin

OXFORD and OXFORD ENGLISH
are trade marks of Oxford University Press

ISBN 0 19 423066 X

This simplified edition © Oxford University Press 2000

Seventh impression 2002

First published in Oxford Bookworms 1989
This second edition published in the Oxford Bookworms Library 2000

A complete recording of this Bookworms edition of *Ghost Stories*
is available on cassette ISBN 0 19 422700 6

The publisher is grateful to the following
for their kind permission to adapt copyright material:
J. S. F. Burrage for *Smee*; A. P. Wyatt Ltd (on behalf of the Executors of K. S. P.
McDowell) for *The Confession of Charles Linkworth*; A. P. Wyatt Ltd (on behalf
of the Rt. Hon. Lord Tweedsmuir of Elsfield C.B.E.) for *Fullcircle*; Dobson
Books Ltd for *The Stranger in the Mist* (originally published as *An Encounter in
the Mist* in the collection *The Alabaster Hand and Other Ghost Stories*).

Please note that *The Ghost Coach* was originally published as *The Phantom Coach*

Illustrated by Alan Marks

Printed in Spain by Unigraf s.l.

CONTENTS

Smee

1

'No,' said Jackson with a shy little smile. 'I'm sorry. I won't play hide and seek.'

It was Christmas Eve, and there were fourteen of us in the house. We had had a good dinner, and we were all in the mood for fun and games – all, that is, except Jackson. When somebody suggested hide and seek, there were loud shouts of agreement. Jackson's refusal was the only one.

It was not like Jackson to refuse to play a game. 'Aren't you feeling well?' someone asked.

'I'm perfectly all right, thank you,' he said. 'But,' he added with a smile that softened his refusal but did not change it, 'I'm still not playing hide and seek.'

'Why not?' someone asked. He hesitated for a moment before replying. 'I sometimes go and stay at a house where a girl was killed. She was playing hide and seek in the dark. She didn't know the house very well. There was a door that led to the servants' staircase. When she was chased, she thought the door led to a bedroom. She opened the door and jumped – and landed at the bottom of the stairs. She broke her neck, of course.'

We all looked serious. Mrs Fernley said, 'How terrible! And were you there when it happened?'

Jackson shook his head sadly. 'No,' he said, 'but I was there when something else happened. Something worse.'

'What could be worse than that?'

1

'This was,' said Jackson. He hesitated for a moment, then he said, 'I wonder if any of you have ever played a game called "Smee". It's much better than hide and seek. The name comes from "It's me", of course. Perhaps you'd like to play it instead of hide and seek. Let me tell you the rules of the game.

'Every player is given a sheet of paper. All the sheets except one are blank. On the last sheet of paper is written "Smee". Nobody knows who "Smee" is except "Smee" himself – or herself. You turn out the lights, and "Smee" goes quietly out of the room and hides. After a time the others go off to search for "Smee" – but of course they don't know who they are looking for. When one player meets another he challenges him by saying, "Smee". The other player answers "Smee", and they continue searching.

'But the real "Smee" doesn't answer when someone challenges. The second player stays quietly beside him. Presently they will be discovered by a third player. He will challenge and receive no answer, and he will join the first two. This goes on until all the players are in the same place. The last one to find "Smee" has to pay a forfeit. It's a good, noisy, amusing game. In a big house it often takes a long time for everyone to find "Smee". Perhaps you'd like to try. I'll happily pay my forfeit and sit here by the fire while you play.'

'It sounds a good game,' I remarked. 'Have you played it too, Jackson?'

'Yes,' he answered. 'I played it in the house that I was telling you about.'

'And *she* was there? The girl who broke — .'

'No, no,' said someone else. 'He told us he wasn't there when she broke her neck.'

Jackson thought for a moment. 'I don't know if she was there or not. I'm afraid she was. I know that there were thirteen of us playing the game, and there were only twelve people in the house. And I didn't know the dead girl's name. When I heard that whispered name in the dark, it didn't worry me. But I tell you, I'm never going to play that kind of game again. It made me quite nervous for a long time. I prefer to pay my forfeit at once!'

We all stared at him. His words did not make sense at all.

Tim Vouce was the kindest man in the world. He smiled at us all.

'This sounds like an interesting story,' he said. 'Come on, Jackson, you can tell it to us instead of paying a forfeit.'

'Very well,' said Jackson. And here is his story.

2

Have you met the Sangstons? They are cousins of mine, and they live in Surrey. Five years ago they invited me to go and spend Christmas with them.

It was an old house, with lots of unnecessary passages and staircases. A stranger could get lost in it quite easily.

Well, I went down for that Christmas. Violet Sangston promised me that I knew most of the other guests. Unfortunately, I couldn't get away from my job until Christmas Eve. All the other guests had arrived there the

3

previous day. I was the last to arrive, and I was only just in time for dinner. I said 'Hullo' to everyone I knew, and Violet Sangston introduced me to the people I didn't know. Then it was time to go in to dinner.

That is perhaps why I didn't hear the name of a tall, dark-haired handsome girl whom I hadn't met before. Everyone was in rather a hurry and I am always bad at catching people's names. She looked cold and clever. She didn't look at all friendly, but she looked interesting, and I wondered who she was. I didn't ask, because I was sure that someone would speak to her by name during the meal. Unluckily, however, I was a long way from her at table. I was sitting next to Mrs Gorman, and as usual Mrs Gorman was being very bright and amusing. Her conversation is always worth listening to, and I completely forgot to ask the name of the dark, proud girl.

There were twelve of us, including the Sangstons themselves. We were all young – or trying to be young. Jack and Violet Sangston were the oldest, and their seventeen-year-old son Reggie was the youngest. It was Reggie who suggested 'Smee' when the talk turned to games. He told us the rules of the game, just as I've described them to you. Jack Sangston warned us all. 'If you are going to play games in the dark,' he said, 'please be careful of the back stairs on the first floor. A door leads to them, and I've often thought about taking the door off. In the dark a stranger to the house could think they were walking into a room. A girl really did break her neck on those stairs.'

I asked how it happened.

'It was about ten years ago, before we came here. There

was a party and they were playing hide and seek. This girl was looking for somewhere to hide. She heard somebody coming, and ran along the passage to get away. She opened the door, thinking it led to a bedroom. She planned to hide in there until the seeker had gone. Unfortunately it was the door that led to the back stairs. She fell straight down to the bottom of the stairs. She was dead when they picked her up.'

We all promised to be careful. Mrs Gorman even made a little joke about living to be ninety. You see, none of us had known the poor girl, and we did not want to feel sad on Christmas Eve.

Well, we all started the game immediately after dinner. Young Reggie Sangston went round making sure all the lights were off, except the ones in the servants' rooms and in the sitting-room where we were. We then prepared twelve sheets of paper. Eleven of them were blank, and one of them had 'Smee' written on it. Reggie mixed them all up, then we each took one. The person who got the paper with 'Smee' on it had to hide. I looked at mine and saw that it was blank. A moment later, all the electric lights went out. In the darkness I heard someone moving very quietly to the door.

After a minute somebody blew a whistle, and we all rushed to the door. I had no idea who was 'Smee'. For five or ten minutes we were all rushing up and down passages and in and out of rooms, challenging each other and answering, 'Smee? – Smee!'.

After a while, the noise died down, and I guessed that someone had found 'Smee'. After a time I found a group of people all sitting on some narrow stairs. I challenged, and received no answer. So 'Smee' was there. I hurriedly joined

We were all rushing up and down passages and in and out of rooms.

the group. Presently two more players arrived. Each one was hurrying to avoid being last. Jack Sangston was last, and was given a forfeit.

'I think we're all here now, aren't we?' he remarked. He lit a match, looked up the staircase and began to count.

'. . . Nine, ten, eleven, twelve, *thirteen*,' he said, and then laughed. 'That's silly – there's one too many!'

The match went out, and he lit another and began to count. He got as far as twelve, then he looked puzzled.

'There are thirteen people here!' he said. 'I haven't counted myself yet.'

'Oh, nonsense!' I laughed. 'You probably began with yourself, and now you want to count yourself twice.'

His son took out his electric torch. It gave a better light than the matches, and we all began to count. Of course there were twelve of us. Jack laughed. 'Well,' he said, 'I was sure I counted thirteen twice.'

From half way up the stairs Violet Sangston spoke nervously. 'I thought there was somebody sitting two steps above me. Have you moved, Captain Ransome?'

The captain said that he hadn't. 'But I thought there was somebody sitting between Mrs Sangston and me.'

Just for a moment there was an uncomfortable *something* in the air. A cold finger seemed to touch us all. For that moment we all felt that something odd and unpleasant had just happened – and was likely to happen again. Then we laughed at ourselves, and at each other, and we felt normal again. There *were* only twelve of us, and that was that. Still laughing, we marched back to the sitting-room to begin again.

3

This time I was 'Smee'. Violet Sangston found me while I was searching for a hiding-place. That game didn't last long. Soon there were twelve people and the game was over. Violet felt cold, and wanted her jacket. Her husband went up to their bedroom to fetch it. As soon as he'd gone, Reggie touched me on the arm. He was looking pale and sick. 'Quick!' he whispered, 'I've got to talk to you. Something horrible has happened.'

We went into the breakfast-room. 'What's the matter?' I asked.

'I don't know. You were "Smee" last time, weren't you? Well, of course I didn't know who "Smee" was. While Mother and the others ran to the west side of the house and found you, I went east. There's a deep clothes cupboard in my bedroom. It looked like a good hiding-place. I thought that perhaps "Smee" might be there. I opened the door in the dark – and touched somebody's hand. "Smee?" I whispered. There was no answer. I thought I'd found "Smee".

'Well, I don't understand it, but I suddenly had a strange, cold feeling. I can't describe it, but I felt that something was wrong. So I turned on my electric torch and there was nobody there. Now, I am sure I touched a hand. And nobody could get out of the cupboard, because I was standing in the doorway. What do you think?'

'You imagined that you touched a hand,' I said.

He gave a short laugh. 'I knew you would say that,' he

said. 'Of course I imagined it. That's the only explanation, isn't it?'

I agreed with him. I could see that he still felt shaken. Together we returned to the sitting-room for another game of 'Smee'. The others were all ready and waiting to start again.

4

Perhaps it was my imagination (although I'm almost sure that it was not). But I had a feeling that nobody was really enjoying the game any more. But everyone was too polite to mention it. All the same, I had the feeling that something was wrong. All the fun had gone out of the game. Something deep inside me was trying to warn me. 'Take care,' it whispered. 'Take care'. There was some unnatural, unhealthy influence at work in the house. Why did I have this feeling? Because Jack Sangston had counted thirteen people instead of twelve? Because his son imagined he had touched someone's hand in an empty cupboard? I tried to laugh at myself, but I did not succeed.

Well, we started again. While we were all chasing the unknown 'Smee' we were all as noisy as ever. But it seemed to me that most of us were just acting. We were no longer enjoying the game. At first I stayed with the others. But for several minutes no 'Smee' was found. I left the main group and started searching on the first floor at the west side of the house. And there, while I was feeling my way along, I bumped into a pair of human knees.

I put out my hand and touched a soft, heavy curtain. Then I knew where I was. There were tall, deep windows with window-seats at the end of the passage. The curtains reached to the ground. Somebody was sitting in a corner of one of the window-seats, behind a curtain.

'Aha!' I thought, 'I've caught "Smee"!' So I pulled the curtain to one side – and touched a woman's arm.

It was a dark, moonless night outside. I couldn't see the woman sitting in the corner of the window-seat.

'Smee?' I whispered.

There was no answer. When 'Smee' is challenged, he – or she – does not answer. So I sat down beside her to wait for the others. Then I whispered, 'What's your name?'

And out of the darkness beside me the whisper came: 'Brenda Ford'.

5

I did not know the name, but I guessed at once who she was. I knew every girl in the house by name except one. And that was the tall, pale, dark girl. So here she was sitting beside me on the window-seat, shut in between a heavy curtain and a window. I was beginning to enjoy the game. I wondered if she was enjoying it too. I whispered one or two rather ordinary questions to her, and received no answer.

'Smee' is a game of silence. It is a rule of the game that 'Smee' and the person or persons who have found 'Smee' have to keep quiet. This, of course, makes it harder for the others to find them. But there was nobody else about. I wondered, therefore, why she was insisting on silence. I spoke again and got no answer. I began to feel a little annoyed. 'Perhaps she is one of those cold, clever girls who have a poor opinion of all men,' I thought. 'She doesn't like me, and she is using the rules of the game as an excuse for not speaking. Well, if she doesn't like sitting here with me, I certainly don't want to sit with her!' I turned away from her. 'I hope someone finds us soon,' I thought.

As I sat there, I realized that I disliked sitting beside this girl very much indeed. That was strange. The girl I had seen at dinner had seemed likeable in a cold kind of way. I noticed her and wanted to know more about her. But now I felt really uncomfortable beside her. The feeling of something wrong, something unnatural, was growing. I remembered touching her arm, and I trembled with horror. I wanted to jump up and run away. I prayed that someone else would come along soon.

Just then I heard light footsteps in the passage. Somebody on the other side of the curtain brushed against my knees. The curtain moved to one side, and a woman's hand touched my shoulder. 'Smee?' whispered a voice that I recognized at once. It was Mrs Gorman. Of course she received no answer. She came and sat down beside me, and at once I felt very much better.

'It's Tony Jackson, isn't it?' she whispered.

'Yes,' I whispered back.

'You're not "Smee", are you?'

'No, she's on my other side.'

She reached out across me. I heard her finger-nails scratch a woman's silk dress. 'Hullo, "Smee". How are you? *Who*

11

The feeling of something wrong, something unnatural, was growing.

are you? Oh, is it against the rules to talk? Never mind, Tony, we'll break the rules. Do you know, Tony, this game is beginning to annoy me a little. I hope they aren't going to play it all evening. I'd like to play a nice quiet game, all together beside a warm fire.'

'Me too,' I agreed.

'Can't you suggest something to them? There's something rather unhealthy about this particular game. I'm sure I'm being very silly. But I can't get rid of the idea that we've got an extra player . . . somebody who ought not to be here at all.'

That was exactly how I felt, but I didn't say so. However, I felt very much better. Mrs Gorman's arrival had chased away my fears. We sat talking. 'I wonder when the others will find us?' said Mrs Gorman.

After a time we heard the sound of feet, and young Reggie's voice shouting, 'Hullo, hullo! Is anybody there?'

'Yes,' I answered.

'Is Mrs Gorman with you?'

'Yes.'

'What happened to you? You've both got forfeits. We've all been waiting for you for hours.'

'But you haven't found "Smee" yet,' I complained.

'*You* haven't, you mean. I was "Smee" this time.'

'But "Smee" is here with us!' I cried.

'Yes,' agreed Mrs Gorman.

The curtain was pulled back and we sat looking into the eye of Reggie's electric torch. I looked at Mrs Gorman, and then on my other side. Between me and the wall was an empty place on the window-seat. I stood up at once. Then I

13

sat down again. I was feeling very sick and the world seemed to be going round and round.

'There *was* somebody there,' I insisted, 'because I touched her.'

'So did I,' said Mrs Gorman, in a trembling voice. 'And I don't think anyone could leave this window-seat without us knowing.'

Reggie gave a shaky little laugh. I remembered his unpleasant experience earlier that evening. 'Someone's been playing jokes,' he said. 'Are you coming down?'

6

We were not very popular when we came down to the sitting-room.

'I found the two of them sitting behind a curtain, on a window-seat,' said Reggie.

I went up to the tall, dark girl.

'So you pretended to be "Smee", and then went away!' I accused her.

She shook her head. Afterwards we all played cards in the sitting-room, and I was very glad.

Some time later, Jack Sangston wanted to talk to me. I could see that he was rather cross with me, and soon he told me the reason.

'Tony,' he said, 'I suppose you are in love with Mrs Gorman. That's your business, but please don't make love to her in my house, during a game. You kept everyone waiting. It was very rude of you, and I'm ashamed of you.'

'But we were not alone!' I protested. 'There was somebody else there – somebody who was pretending to be "Smee". I believe it was that tall, dark girl, Miss Ford. She whispered her name to me. Of course, she refused to admit it afterwards.'

Jack Sangston stared at me. 'Miss *who?*' he breathed.

'Brenda Ford, she said.'

Jack put a hand on my shoulder. 'Look here, Tony,' he said, 'I don't mind a joke, but enough is enough. We don't want to worry the ladies. Brenda Ford is the name of the girl who broke her neck on the stairs. She was playing hide and seek here ten years ago.'

The Judge's House

1

It was April and John Moore was studying for an important examination. As the date of the exam came nearer, he decided to go somewhere and read by himself. He did not want the amusements of the seaside, or the beauties of the countryside. He decided to find a quiet, ordinary little town and work there undisturbed. He packed his suitcases with clothes and books. Then he looked in a railway timetable for a town that he did not know. He found one, and bought a ticket to go there. He did not tell anyone where he was going. After all, he did not want to be disturbed.

That is how Moore arrived at Benchurch. It was a market town, and once a week it was quite busy for a few hours. The rest of the time it was a very quiet, sleepy little place. Moore spent his first night at the only hotel in the town. The landlady was very kind and helpful, but the hotel was not really quiet enough for him. The second day he started looking for a house to rent.

There was only one place that he liked. It was more than quiet – it was deserted and very lonely. It was a big, old seventeenth-century house. It had tiny windows like a prison, and a high brick wall all round it. It would be hard to imagine a more unwelcoming place. But it suited Moore perfectly. He went to find the local lawyer, who was responsible for the house.

Mr Carnford, the lawyer, was very happy to rent the house to him.

'I'd be glad to let you have it free,' he said, 'just to have somebody living in it again after all these years. It's been empty so long that people have spread a lot of foolish stories about it. You'll be able to prove that the stories are wrong.'

Moore did not think it was necessary to ask the lawyer for more details of the 'foolish stories'. He paid his rent, and Mr Carnford gave him the name of an old servant to look after him. He came away from the lawyer's office with the keys of the house in his pocket. He then went to Mrs Wood, the landlady of the hotel.

'I'm renting a house for a few weeks,' he said. 'Can you advise me about shopping, please? What do you think I shall need?'

'Where are you going to stay, sir?' the landlady asked. Moore told her.

She threw up her hands in horror. 'Not the Judge's House!' she said, and she grew pale as she spoke.

He asked her to tell him more about the house. 'Why is it called the Judge's House?' he said, 'and why doesn't anyone want to live in it?'

2

'Well, sir,' she said, 'a long time ago – no, I don't know how long – a judge lived there. He was a hard, cruel judge, sir – a real hanging judge. He showed no mercy to anyone. But as for the house itself – well, I can't

17

say. I've often asked, but nobody could tell me for certain.'
She found it hard to explain. The general feeling in the town
was that there was something strange about the Judge's
House. 'As for me, sir,' she said, 'I won't stay there alone,
not for all the money in the bank!'

Then she apologized to Moore. 'I'm sorry to worry you,
sir, really I am. But if you were my son I wouldn't let you
stay there one night on your own. I'd go there myself and
pull the big alarm bell that's on the roof!'

Moore was grateful for her kindness and her anxiety.
'How good of you to be so anxious about me, Mrs Wood!'
he said. 'But there's really no need to worry. I'm studying
for an important examination and I have no time for
horrors or mysteries.'

The landlady kindly promised to do his shopping for him.
Moore then went to see the old servant whom Mr Carnford
had recommended to him. Her name was Mrs Dempster,
and she seemed pleasant and eager to please her new master.

When he returned with her to the Judge's House two
hours later, he found Mrs Wood waiting outside it. She had
several people with her – men and boys carrying parcels,
and another two men with a bed.

'But there are beds in the house!' cried Moore in surprise.

'And nobody's slept in them for fifty years or more! No,
sir, I won't let you risk your life in an old, damp bed.'

The landlady was obviously curious to see the inside of
the house. At the same time she was clearly afraid. At the
smallest noise she held nervously to Moore's arm. Together
they explored the whole house. After his exploration,
Moore decided to live in the dining-room. It was big enough

for both working and sleeping. Mrs Wood and Mrs Dempster began to arrange everything. Soon the baskets were unpacked. Moore saw that kind Mrs Wood had brought many good things from her own kitchen. Before she left she turned to Moore and said, 'I do hope you will be all right, sir. But I must say – I couldn't sleep here, with all those ghosts!'

When she left, Mrs Dempster laughed. 'Ghosts!' she said. 'Ghosts! There *are* no ghosts! There are rats and insects, and doors that need oiling. There are windows that blow open in the wind. . . . Look at the old oak walls of this room, sir. They are old – hundreds of years old! Don't you think there'll be rats and insects behind the wood? You'll see plenty of rats here, sir, but you won't see any ghosts – I'm sure of that. Now you go and have a nice walk, sir. And when you come back, I'll have this room all ready for you.'

She kept her promise. When Moore returned he found the room clean and neat. A fire was burning in the ancient fireplace. She had lit the lamp and put his supper ready on the table.

'Good night, sir,' she said. 'I have to go now and get my husband's supper. I'll see you in the morning.'

'This is wonderful!' said Moore to himself as he ate Mrs Dempster's excellent food. When he had finished his supper, he pushed the dishes to the other end of the table. He put more wood on the fire and began to study.

3

Moore worked without stopping until about eleven o'clock. Then he put some more wood on the fire. He also made a pot of tea. He was enjoying himself very much. The fire was burning brightly. The firelight danced on the old oak walls and threw strange shadows around the room. His tea tasted excellent, and there was nobody to disturb him. Then for the first time he noticed how much noise the rats were making.

'Were they making all this noise while I was studying?' he thought. 'No, I don't think they were. Perhaps they were afraid of me at first. Now they have become braver, and they are running about as usual.'

How busy they were! And what a lot of noise they made! Up and down they rushed, behind the old oak walls, over the ceiling and under the floor. Moore remembered Mrs Dempster's words: 'You'll see plenty of rats, but you won't see any ghosts.' 'Well,' he said with a smile, 'she was right about the rats, anyway!'

He picked up the lamp and looked around the room. 'How strange,' he said to himself. 'Why doesn't anybody want to live in this beautiful old house?' The oak walls were very beautiful. There were some old pictures on the walls, but they were covered with dust and dirt and he could not see them clearly. Here and there he saw small holes in the walls. From time to time the curious face of a rat stared at him. Then with a scratch and a squeak, it was gone.

The thing that interested him most, however, was the

rope of the great alarm bell on the roof. The rope hung down in a corner of the room on the right-hand side of the fireplace. He found a huge, high-backed oak chair and pulled it up beside the fire. There he sat and drank his last cup of tea. Then he put more wood on the fire and sat down at the table again with his books. For a time the rats disturbed him with their scratching and squeaking. But he got used to the noise, and soon he forgot everything except his work.

Suddenly he looked up. Something had disturbed him, but he did not know what it was. He sat up and listened. The room was silent. That was it! The noise of the rats had stopped. 'That's what disturbed me!' said Moore with a smile. He looked around the room – and saw an enormous rat. It was sitting on the great high-backed chair by the fire, and it was staring at him with hate in its small red eyes. Moore picked up a book and pretended to throw it. But the rat did not move. It showed its great white teeth angrily, and its cruel eyes shone mercilessly in the lamplight.

'Why, you — ' cried Moore. He picked up the poker from the fireplace and jumped up. Before he could hit the rat, however, it jumped to the floor with a squeak. It ran up the rope of the alarm bell and disappeared in the darkness. Strangely, the squeaks and scratches of the rats in the walls began again.

By this time Moore no longer felt like working. Outside the house the birds were singing: soon it would be morning. He climbed into bed and immediately fell asleep.

4

He slept so deeply that he did not hear Mrs Dempster come in. She dusted the room and made his breakfast. Then she woke him with a cup of tea.

After breakfast he put a book in his pocket and went out for a walk. On the way he bought a few sandwiches. ('Then I shan't have to stop for lunch,' he said to himself). He found a pretty, quiet little park and spent most of the day there, studying. On his way home he called at the hotel to thank Mrs Wood for her kindness. She looked at him searchingly.

'You must not work too hard, sir. You look pale this morning. Too much studying isn't good for anyone. But tell me, sir, did you have a good night? Mrs Dempster told me you were still asleep when she went in.'

'Oh, I was all right,' said Moore with a smile. 'The ghosts haven't troubled me yet. But the rats had a party last night! There was one old devil with red eyes. He sat up on the chair by the fire. He didn't move until I picked up the poker. Then he ran up the rope of the alarm bell. I didn't see where he went. It was too dark.'

'Dear God!' cried Mrs Wood, 'an old devil sitting by the fire! Take care, sir, take care.'

'What do you mean?' asked Moore in surprise.

'An old devil! *The* old devil, perhaps.' Moore started to laugh.

'Please forgive me, Mrs Wood,' he said at last. 'I just couldn't help laughing at the idea of the Devil himself sitting

There, in the Judge's chair, sat the rat, staring at him with hate in its small red eyes.

by my fire . . . ' And he began to laugh again. Then he went home for dinner.

That evening the noise of the rats began earlier. After dinner he sat down beside the fire and drank his tea. Then he sat down at the table and started to work again.

The rats disturbed him more than the previous night. They scratched and squeaked and ran about, and stared at him from the holes in the walls. Their eyes shone like tiny lamps in the firelight. But Moore was becoming used to them. They seemed playful rather than aggressive. Sometimes the bravest rats ran out onto the floor or across the tops of the pictures. Now and again, when they disturbed him, Moore shook his papers at them. They ran to their holes at once. And so the early part of the night passed quite quietly.

Moore worked hard for several hours.

All at once he was disturbed by a sudden silence. There was not a sound of running, or scratching, or squeaking. The huge room was as silent as the grave. Moore remembered the previous night. He looked at the chair by the fireside – and got a terrible shock. There, on the great high-backed oak chair, sat the same enormous rat. It was staring at him with hate.

Without thinking, Moore picked up the nearest book and threw it. It missed, and the rat did not move. So Moore again picked up the poker. Again the rat ran up the rope of the alarm bell. And once more the other rats started their scratching and squeaking. Moore was unable to see where the rat had gone. The light of the lamp did not reach as far as the high ceiling, and the fire had burned low.

Moore looked at his watch. It was almost midnight. He put more wood on the fire and made a pot of tea. Then he sat down in the great oak chair by the fire and enjoyed his tea.

'I wonder where that old rat went just now,' he thought. 'I must buy a rat trap in the morning.' He lit another lamp. He placed it so that it would shine into the right-hand corner of the wall by the fireplace. He got several books ready to throw at the creature. Finally he lifted the rope of the alarm bell. He put it on the table and fixed the end of it under the lamp.

As he handled the rope, Moore noticed how pliable it was. 'You could hang a man with it,' he thought. Then he stood back and admired his preparations.

'There, my friend,' he said aloud, 'I think I'll learn your secret this time!'

He started work again, and was soon lost in his studies. But once again he was disturbed by a sudden silence. Then the bell rope moved a little, and the lamp on top of the rope moved too. Moore made sure that his books were ready for throwing. Then he looked along the rope. As he looked, the great rat dropped from the rope onto the old oak chair. It sat there staring at him angrily. He picked up a book and aimed it at the rat. The creature jumped cleverly to one side. Moore threw another book, but without success. Then, as Moore stood with a third book in his hand, ready to throw, the rat squeaked and seemed to be afraid. Moore threw the book and it hit the rat's side. With a squeak of pain and fear, and a look of real hate, it ran up the back of the chair and made a great jump onto the rope of the alarm bell. It ran up the rope like lightning, while the heavy lamp shook with its desperate speed. Moore watched the rat carefully. By the light of the second lamp, he saw it disappear through a hole in one of the great pictures on the wall.

'I shall check my unpleasant little visitor's home in the morning,' said Moore to himself as he picked up his books from the floor. 'The third picture from the fireplace: I shan't forget.' He examined the books. He picked up the third book that he had thrown. 'This is the one that hurt him!' he said to himself. Then his face turned pale. 'Why – it's my mother's old Bible! How strange!' He sat down to work again, and once more the rats in the walls started their noise. This did not worry him. Compared with the huge rat, these ones seemed almost friendly. But he could not work. At last he closed his books and went to bed. The first red light of morning was shining through the window as he closed his eyes.

5

He slept heavily but uneasily, and he had unpleasant dreams. Then Mrs Dempster woke him as usual with a cup of tea, and he felt better. But his first request to her surprised the old servant very much. 'Mrs Dempster, while I'm out today, will you please dust or wash those pictures – particularly the third one from the fireplace. I want to see what they are.'

Again Moore spent most of the day studying happily in

the park. On his way home he again visited Mrs Wood at the hotel. She had a visitor with her in her comfortable sitting-room.

'Sir,' said the landlady, 'this is Doctor Thornhill.'

As soon as she had introduced them, the doctor began to ask Moore a great many questions. 'I'm sure,' said Moore to himself, 'that the good doctor did not call here by accident.' He turned to Doctor Thornhill.

'Doctor, I'll gladly answer all your questions, if you'll just answer one of mine.'

The doctor seemed surprised, but he agreed at once.

'Did Mrs Wood ask you to come here and advise me?' asked Moore. The doctor looked surprised. Mrs Wood's face turned very red and she looked away. But the doctor was an honest, friendly man, and he answered quickly, 'She did, but she didn't want you to know. She's worried about you. She doesn't like you staying there all alone, and she thinks you study too hard and drink too much strong tea. She asked me to give you some good advice. I was once a student too, you know, so I know what I'm talking about.'

Moore smiled and held out his hand to Doctor Thornhill. 'I must thank you for your kindness – and you too, Mrs Wood. I promise to take no more strong tea, and I'll be in bed by one o'clock. There, will that please you both?'

'Very much,' said Doctor Thornhill. 'Now tell us all about that old house.'

Moore told them all about the events of the previous nights. When he told them how he had thrown the Bible, Mrs Wood gave a little scream. When Moore had finished his story, Doctor Thornhill looked very serious.

27

'The rat always ran up the rope of the alarm bell?' he asked.

'Always.'

'I suppose you know,' said the doctor, 'what the rope is?'

'No, I don't,' said Moore.

'It is the hangman's rope,' said the doctor. 'After the judge condemned someone to death, the unfortunate man was hanged with that rope.' Mrs Wood gave another scream. The doctor went to fetch her a glass of water. When he returned, he looked hard at Moore. 'Listen, young man,' he said. 'If anything happens to you tonight, don't hesitate to ring the alarm bell. I shall be working quite late tonight too, and I'll keep my ears open. Now don't forget!'

Moore laughed. 'I'm sure I shan't need to do that!' he said, and went home for his dinner.

'I don't like that young man's story,' said Doctor Thornhill after Moore had left. 'Perhaps he imagined most of it. All the same, I'll listen tonight for the alarm bell. Perhaps we'll reach him in time to help him.'

6

When Moore arrived home, Mrs Dempster had already left. But his supper was ready for him. The lamp was burning brightly and there was a good fire in the fireplace. It was a cold, windy evening, but the room was warm and inviting. For a few minutes after he came in, the rats were quiet. But, as before, they soon became used to his presence in the room. Soon they started their noise again.

He was glad to hear them. He remembered how silent they had been when the great rat appeared. Moore soon forgot the squeaking and scratching. He sat down to his dinner with a light heart. After dinner he opened his books, determined to get some work done.

For an hour or two he worked very well. Then his concentration weakened, and he looked up. It was a stormy night. The whole house seemed to shake, and the wind whistled down the chimneys with a strange, unnatural sound. The force of the wind shook the alarm bell. The pliable rope rose and fell a little, and the bottom of it hit the oak floor with a hard and hollow sound.

As Moore watched it, he remembered the doctor's words: 'It's the hangman's rope.' He went over to the corner by the fireplace and took the rope in his hand. He looked at it very hard. He wondered how many people had died on the end of that rope. As he held it, the movement of the bell on the roof still lifted it now and again. Then he felt a new movement. The rope seemed to tremble, as if something was moving along it. At the same time, the noise of the rats stopped.

Moore looked up, and saw the great rat coming down towards him. It was staring at him with hate. Moore dropped the rope and jumped back with a cry. The rat turned, ran up the rope again and disappeared. At the same moment Moore realized that the noise of the other rats had begun again.

'Very well, my friend,' thought Moore, 'let's investigate your hiding place.'

He lit the other lamp. He remembered that the rat had

disappeared inside the third picture on the right. He picked up the lamp and carried it across to the picture.

He almost dropped the lamp. He stepped back at once, and the sweat of fear was upon his pale face. His knees shook. His whole body trembled like a leaf. But he was young and brave, and he moved forward again with his lamp. Mrs Dempster had dusted and washed the picture, and Moore could now see it quite clearly.

It showed a judge. He had a cruel, clever, merciless face, with a big curved nose and very bright, hard eyes. As Moore looked into those eyes, he realized that he had seen that look before. The great rat's eyes were exactly the same. They held the same look of hate and cruelty. Then the noise of the rats stopped again, and Moore became conscious of another pair of eyes looking at him. The great rat was staring at him from the hole in the corner of the picture. But Moore took no notice of the creature and continued to examine the picture.

The Judge was sitting in a great, high-backed oak chair, on the right-hand side of a great stone fireplace. In the corner a rope hung down from the ceiling. With a feeling of horror, Moore recognized the room where he now stood. He looked around him, as if he expected to see another presence there. Then he looked across to the corner of the fireplace. He froze with fear and the lamp fell from his trembling hand.

There, in the Judge's chair, sat the rat. The rope hung behind, exactly as it did in the picture. The rat looked at Moore with the same merciless stare as the Judge in the picture. But there was a new, triumphant look in the small red eyes. Everything was silent except for the storm outside.

30

'The lamp!' thought Moore desperately. Fortunately it was a metal one, and the oil had not caught fire. However, he had to put it out. In doing so, he forgot his fears for a moment.

Then he stopped and thought. 'I can't go on like this,' he said to himself. 'The doctor is right. Late hours and strong tea are no good for me. They just make me nervous. However, I'm all right now.' He made himself a warm, milky drink and sat down to work.

Nearly an hour later a sudden silence disturbed him again. Outside, the storm was growling and whistling as loudly as ever. The rain drummed on the windows. But inside the house everything was as quiet as the grave. Moore listened carefully, and then he heard a strange squeaking noise. It came from the corner of the room where the rope hung down. At first he thought the rope itself was making the sound. Then he looked up and saw the great rat. It was chewing the rope with its ugly yellow teeth. It had almost bitten through it, and, as Moore watched, part of the rope fell to the floor. Only a short piece was still attached to the bell, and the rat was still hanging onto it. Now the rope began to swing backwards and forwards. Moore felt a moment of terrible fear. 'Now I can never ring the alarm bell,' he thought. Then he was filled with anger. He picked up the book he was reading, and threw it violently at the rat. He aimed it well. But before the book could hit the creature, it dropped off the rope and landed on the floor. At once Moore rushed towards it, but the rat ran away and disappeared into the shadows.

'Let's have another rat hunt before bed!' said Moore to

himself. He picked up the lamp – and almost dropped it again.

The figure of the Judge had disappeared from the picture. The chair and the details of the room were still there. But the man himself had gone. Frozen with horror, Moore moved slowly round. He began to shake and tremble. His strength left him, and he was unable to move a muscle. He could only see and hear.

There, on the great high-backed oak chair sat the Judge. His merciless eyes stared at Moore. There was a smile of triumph on his cruel mouth. Slowly he lifted up a black hat. Moore's heart was drumming wildly. There was a strange singing noise in his ears. Outside, the wind was as wild as ever. Then, above the screams of the wind, he heard the great clock striking in the market place. He stood and listened, stiff and unmoving. The triumph on the Judge's face grew. As the clock struck twelve, the Judge placed the black hat on his head. Slowly and deliberately, he rose from his chair and picked up the piece of rope from the floor. He pulled it through his hands. Slowly and carefully he made the thick, pliable rope into a noose. He tested the noose with his foot. He pulled hard at it until he was pleased with it. Then he began to move slowly and carefully past the table, on the opposite side to Moore. Then with one quick movement he stood in front of the door. Moore was trapped! All this time, the Judge's eyes never left Moore's.

7

Moore stared into the cruel eyes, like a bird watching a cat. He saw the Judge coming nearer with his noose. He saw him throw the noose towards him. Desperately Moore threw himself to one side, and saw the rope fall harmlessly to the floor. Again the Judge raised the noose and tried to catch Moore. Again and again he tried. And all the time he stared mercilessly at the student. 'He's just playing with me,' thought Moore, 'like a cat playing with a bird. Soon he'll catch me, and hang me . . . '

He looked desperately behind him. Hundreds of rats were watching him with bright, anxious little eyes. Then he saw that the rope of the alarm bell was covered with rats. As he watched, more and more were pouring down onto the rope, from the round hole in the ceiling that led to the bell itself. The rats were hanging from the rope, and there were so many of them that the rope was swinging backwards and forwards.

The alarm bell began to ring, softly at first, then more strongly. At the sound, the Judge looked up. A devilish anger spread across his face. His eyes burned like red jewels. Outside there was a sudden, deafening crash of thunder. The Judge raised his noose again, while the rats ran desperately up and down the rope of the alarm bell.

This time, instead of throwing the rope, the Judge moved nearer to Moore, and held the noose open. Moore was unable to move. He stood there like a stone figure. He felt the Judge's icy fingers and the pliable rope against his neck.

He felt the noose against his throat. Then the Judge picked up the stiff body of the student in his arms. He carried him over to the great oak chair and stood him on it. Then, stepping up beside him, the Judge put up his hand and caught the rope of the alarm bell. At his touch the rats ran away, squeaking with fear. They disappeared through the hole in the ceiling. Then the Judge took the end of the noose which was around Moore's neck. He tied it to the hanging bell rope. Then he climbed down, and pulled away the chair.

8

When the alarm bell of the Judge's House began to ring, a crowd soon gathered. People came running with lanterns and torches, and soon hundreds of people were hurrying to the house. They knocked loudly at the door, but there was no reply. Then they broke down the door, and poured into the great dining-room. The Doctor was the first to reach Moore. But too late.

There at the end of the bell rope hung the body of the student. The Judge stared out once more from his picture. But on his face there was a smile of triumph.

There at the end of the bell rope hung the body of the student.

The Stranger in the Mist

1

Giles Hampton was spending a short holiday in Wales. A friend of his had recently sold his business in Liverpool and had moved to Wales. This friend, whose name was Beverley, had built himself a house in Caernarvonshire, near the Snowdon mountains. There was an ancient church called Fablan Fawr a few hundred yards away from his house, so Beverley called his new house Fablan Fawr too.

Giles was very interested in geology. He loved studying rocks and stones. Since that part of Wales is of particular interest to the geologist, Giles was very glad indeed to receive Beverley's invitation to visit him. Giles arrived at Fablan Fawr on the evening of October 10. The house was very modern and extremely comfortable. It stood between the mountains and the Conway Valley. A few hundred yards behind the house lay the steep, rocky mountains.

The weather was fine, and for the first week of his stay Giles went with Beverley on several short geological expeditions. They also went shooting together once or twice, and they visited neighbours in the district. But on October 18 Beverley had business in the local market town. So Giles decided to make an all-day excursion to a place on the other side of the mountains, about ten miles away. The sky was cloudy when Giles set off after an early breakfast. In his bag were his sandwiches and his geological hammers, and information from Beverley's servant, Parry, about his route across the mountains.

It was after twelve o'clock when Giles arrived and began unpacking his hammers. The sun had come out, and he was hot, tired and uncomfortable. But he soon forgot his discomfort when he examined the many interesting rocks. It was half-past three before he had finished. He packed his hammers and notebook away in his bag again and started on the journey back to Fablan Fawr. By this time the sky was cloudy again. As he walked along, light rain began to fall. Then, as he climbed higher, a thick, damp mist came down and covered everything. Soon the mist grew thicker and he could see only a few feet in front of him.

On his earlier journey across the mountains Giles had looked out for landmarks – a waterfall, an old tree, a small lake. He thought these would help him to find his way back to Fablan Fawr. But in the mist everything looked strange and different. Soon he crossed a stream which he did not recognize. Then he knew that he had taken the wrong path.

For nearly half a mile he went back the way he had come, only to become more lost and confused than before.

'This is no good,' he thought. He sat down for a few moments to consider his position. The thought of a cold, uncomfortable night alone on the hillside did not particularly worry him. But he knew that Beverley would be very anxious. Giles did not want to worry his friend. 'He'll come out to search for me,' thought Giles, 'and bring the neighbours too. I can't let him organize a search party. I really can't.'

2

S uddenly he heard the sound of footsteps on the hillside above him. He shouted, and a voice answered him in Welsh. From out of the mist came an old man with a huge dog by his side. Although the man was old, he stood straight and tall. He wore a heavy cloak of dark cloth that came down to his ankles. He wore no hat and his hair was long and white. His big red face shone with kindness.

The old man spoke again in Welsh. Giles made signs to show that he did not understand. The old man smiled kindly. 'I'm lost,' said Giles, making more signs. 'I want to go to Fablan Fawr.'

The old man seemed to understand. 'Fablan Fawr,' he repeated several times, and smiled again. Then he felt inside his long cloak and pulled out a map. He spread the map out on a stone in front of him.

Beverley's new house was not, of course, on the map. But the church of Fablan Fawr was clearly shown. With his thin old hand the stranger pointed to a place on the map. He spoke again in Welsh, then pointed again. 'He is telling me that we are here,' said Giles to himself. Then the old man pointed out the path that Giles must take to reach Fablan Fawr. He did this three times, to make sure that Giles understood. Then he pushed the map into Giles's hands. Giles tried to refuse this gift, but the old man only laughed and smiled. Giles thanked him warmly and pushed the map into his coat pocket. Then he set out along the path that the old man had shown him. After a few steps he turned. He

From out of the mist came an old man with a huge dog by his side.

saw a shape through the mist, standing and watching him. He waved his hand and set off again. The next time he turned round, the old man had disappeared.

Giles walked fast. The mist had become thicker than before, but the path was a good one. From time to time he checked his route on the map. Soon the path led him down a very steep hillside. In the mist, Giles could see only a few feet ahead, so he moved very carefully. Suddenly his foot turned on a sharp stone and he almost fell. That stone probably saved his life. It flew up from under his feet and rolled down the steep path. He heard it rolling faster and faster, then the noise stopped. A few seconds later Giles heard a crash as the stone hit the ground hundreds of feet below. The path had led him to the edge of a cliff! Giles picked up another stone and dropped it. Again he heard the distant crash as it fell over the cliff. He looked at the map again. There was no cliff on the route that the old man had shown him. For the first time, Giles became seriously worried. He sat down miserably on a large rock, took out his pipe, and found a match to light it. 'Well,' he thought, 'I'll just have to sit and wait for the mist to clear.'

3

Perhaps it was an hour later when he heard a voice shouting on the hillside below. Giles shouted back as loudly as he could. Slowly the shouts got nearer. He recognized the voice of Beverley's servant, Parry, who had become anxious about Giles's safety, and had set out to search for him. Beverley himself had not returned from the town. Giles was extremely grateful for this: he hated to trouble his friend.

Parry led Giles safely back towards the house. Giles walked slowly and quietly, thankful to be rescued. But for some reason he was unwilling to tell Parry about the stranger in the mist. He explained that he had taken the wrong path. In less than an hour he was changing his wet clothes.

At dinner, too, he kept quiet about it, simply telling Beverley that he had lost his way in the mist.

'I suppose I took the wrong path,' he said, 'and I found myself at the edge of a cliff.'

'You had a very lucky escape,' said Beverley. 'There have been some nasty accidents in these hills. A man was killed about four years ago. I believe he was found at the bottom of the same cliff. That was before I came here, of course.' He turned to his servant. 'I'm sure you remember the accident, Parry,' he said. 'Am I right? Was it the same place?'

'It certainly was, sir,' said the servant. 'It was a gentleman from London. They buried him in the churchyard here. I was working for Captain Trevor at that time. He let us all go to the burial. Mr Roberts buried him and prayed over the grave. It was all in the local newspaper. I kept the newspaper – it was the *Caernarvon and District News*. I'll fetch it if you like, sir.'

'That's a good idea, Parry,' said his master. In a few minutes Parry returned with an old newspaper. Beverley read the report aloud:

'Early on Wednesday morning the body of a young man

41

was found at the bottom of the cliff at Adwy-yr-Eryon. A doctor examined the body and decided that the man had been dead for several hours. The unfortunate man was Mr John Stevenson, a young lawyer from London. Mr Stevenson had been on holiday in Wales, and he had been exploring our beautiful mountains and valleys. When he did not return to his hotel in the evening, Captain Trevor, a local man, bravely organized a search party. Unfortunately, the thick mist made their work more difficult.

It appears that the dead man took the wrong path in the mist, and fell over the cliff, hitting the sharp rocks below. In the dead man's pocket was a copy of a very old, out-of-date map. It showed a long-disused path over the hill. Of course, as everyone in the district knows, the path was destroyed many years ago by the Great Landslide. That was a terrible disaster which carried away a large part of the hillside.

The sad death of Mr Stevenson should be a warning to everyone. Never depend on an out-of-date map. A modern, accurate map of the district is available from the offices of this newspaper, price nine pence.'

4

When Giles heard about the out-of-date map in the dead man's pocket, he was very excited. He told Beverley the whole story of the stranger in the mist. Beverley was very interested.

'Do you remember anything about a map, Parry?' he asked his servant.

'I certainly do, sir,' said Parry. 'It was a very old map. Mr Roberts still has it, I believe.'

'Then will you please send a message to Mr Roberts for me?' said Beverley. 'Give him my best wishes, and ask him to come and have coffee with us. And ask him to bring the old map with him, please.' Parry hurried away to carry out his master's orders.

'I have the map that the old man gave me today,' said Giles. 'It is still in my coat pocket. I'll go and get it.'

He fetched the map and spread it out on the table. The two men studied it carefully. In the mist Giles had not noticed anything strange about the map. But in the brightly lit dining-room the map looked very unusual indeed. It was on thick paper that looked yellow with age. The writing was very old, with long Ss that looked like Fs.

'Look at that!' said Beverley, pointing to some writing at the bottom of the map. 'Madog ap Rhys, 1707.'

Just then Mr Roberts arrived. He listened carefully to Giles's story. Then he took a map out of his pocket. It was exactly like the map that lay on the table.

'I've always wondered how the dead man got that map,' he said. 'It's very unusual. There is only one other copy, and that's in the museum in Caernarvon.'

'And who was Madog ap Rhys?' asked Giles.

'He was a rather strange, lonely old man,' said Mr Roberts. 'He lived alone on the hillside and spent most of his time praying. He died in 1720. Of course that was before the landslide destroyed the path to Adwy-yr-Eryon. When-ever there was a mist, Madog ap Rhys walked among the hills in his long dark cloak, with his dog beside him. He

43

drew this map. He always carried a copy about with him, to give to travellers who had lost their way. Some local people say that his spirit still walks among the hills, searching for lost travellers. But that's only a story. I don't take it very seriously.'

'How sad!' said Giles, after Mr Roberts had drunk his coffee and left. 'Madog ap Rhys was a good, kind man. He only wanted to help. But he led poor Stevenson to his death, and he almost killed me.'

The Confession of Charles Linkworth

1

Doctor Teesdale visited the condemned man in prison once or twice during the week before he was put to death. Condemned men often find a strange peace as the hour of their death comes closer. Linkworth was like this. While there was still hope of saving his life, Linkworth had experienced horrible doubts and fears. When all hope had gone, he seemed to accept that his death was certain, and he became calm and quiet. The murder had been a particularly horrible one, and no one felt sympathetic towards the murderer. The condemned man owned a small paper shop in Sheffield, in the north of England. He lived there with his wife and his mother. The old lady was not rich, but she had five hundred pounds, and Linkworth knew this. Linkworth himself needed money because he owed a hundred pounds, and he simply killed his mother for her money. While his wife was away from home visiting some relations, Linkworth strangled his mother.

He and his mother had had many arguments and disagreements over the past few years. She had often threatened to take her money and go and live somewhere else. In fact, during his wife's absence, Linkworth and his mother had another violent argument. The old lady took all her money out of the bank and made plans to leave Sheffield the next day. She told her son that she was going to live with friends in London. He saw his chance, and that evening he strangled her. During the night he buried the body in the small back garden behind the shop.

His next step, before his wife's return, was a very sensible one. The next morning he packed up all his mother's clothes. He took them down to the station and sent them off to London by passenger train. In the evening he invited several friends to supper, and told them about his mother's departure. He openly admitted that he and his mother had never really agreed with each other. He said that he was not sorry that she had left. He added that she had not given him her London address. That too seemed quite natural, but it was a clever idea all the same. Linkworth did not want his wife to write to the old lady.

When his wife returned, Linkworth told her the same believable story and she accepted it completely. Indeed, this is not surprising, for there was nothing strange or unusual about it. And for a while everything went very well. At first Linkworth was clever. He did not pay the money he owed immediately. Instead, he took a paying guest into his house. This young man rented the old lady's room. At the same time Linkworth mentioned to everyone how he was making money from his little shop. It was a month before he used any of the money from the locked drawer in his mother's room. Then he changed two fifty-pound notes and paid back the money that he owed.

At that point, however, he became careless. Instead of being patient, he paid another two hundred pounds into the bank. And he began to worry about the body in the garden. Was it buried deeply enough? He bought some rocks and stones, and spent the long summer evenings building a rock garden over the grave. The flowers grew, and he began to feel safer and more confident.

But then something quite unexpected happened. His mother's luggage had arrived at Kings Cross Station in London, and of course nobody collected it. It was sent to the lost-luggage office to wait for its owner. It waited and waited – until there was a fire at the office. The old lady's luggage was partly destroyed, and the railway company wrote to her about it at her Sheffield address.

The letter was of course addressed to Mrs Linkworth, and naturally Linkworth's wife opened it. That letter was the beginning of the end for Linkworth. Why was his mother's luggage still in the lost-luggage office? He could give no reasonable explanation. Of course he had to call the police and tell them his mother was missing. Then the silent, slow machinery of English law began to move. Quiet men in dark suits visited Linkworth's shop. They enquired at his bank, and inspected the rock garden behind his shop. Then came the arrest, and the trial, which did not last very long.

Finally, the last day of the trial arrived. Well-dressed ladies in large hats came along to hear the judgement, and the room was bright with colour. No one in the crowd felt sorry for the young man who was condemned. Many of the audience were mothers themselves. The prisoner's crime, they felt, was a crime against motherhood. They felt pleased when the judge put on his black hat. They understood what the black hat meant, and they agreed with the judge. The man was a murderer, and the judge was right to condemn him to death.

2

Linkworth went to his death with a calm, expressionless face. Mr Dawkins, the prison chaplain, did his best to persuade Linkworth to confess his crime. Linkworth refused to admit his guilt. Now, on a bright September morning, the sun shone warmly on the terrible little group that crossed the prison yard. The chaplain prayed. Then the prison officers put a black cloth over the condemned man's head. They tied his arms behind his back. Then they led Linkworth to the hanging-shed to punish him for his crime.

It was Doctor Teesdale's job afterwards to make sure that the man was dead. He did so. He had seen it all, of course. He had heard the chaplain praying. He had watched the prison officers putting the rope around the condemned man's neck. He had seen the floor open up underneath him, and he had watched the body drop down into the black hole below. He had looked down and watched the body trembling and kicking. That lasted for only a few moments; it was a perfect death. An hour later it was Teesdale's duty to examine the body, and again everything was normal. The prisoner's neck was broken; death had been quick and painless. As he examined the body, Teesdale had a very strange feeling. It seemed to him that the spirit of the dead man was very near to him. But the body was cold and stiff. Linkworth had been dead for an hour.

Then another strange thing happened. One of the prison officers came into the room.

'Excuse me, Doctor,' he said politely. 'Has someone

The sun shone warmly on the terrible little group that crossed the prison yard.

brought the rope in here with the body? As you know, the hangman is always allowed to keep the rope, and we can't find it anywhere.'

'No,' said Teesdale in surprise. 'It isn't here. Have you looked in the hanging-shed?'

He thought no more about it. The disappearance of the rope, although it was strange, was not particularly important.

Doctor Teesdale was unmarried, and had a good income of his own. He lived in a pleasing little flat some distance away from the prison. An excellent couple – Mr and Mrs Parker – looked after him. He did not need the money that he earned as a doctor. But he was interested in crime and criminals. That evening Teesdale could not stop thinking about Linkworth.

'It was a horrible crime,' he thought. 'The man did not desperately need the money. It was an unnatural crime: was the man mad? They said at the trial that he was a kind husband, a good neighbour – why did he suddenly do this terrible thing? And afterwards he never confessed. He never asked for forgiveness. Everyone knew that he was guilty; why didn't he confess?'

About half past nine that evening, after one of Mrs Parker's excellent dinners, Teesdale sat alone in his study. Once more he had the feeling of another presence, a strange spirit, in the room. Teesdale was not particularly surprised. 'If the spirit continues to live after the death of the body,' he said to himself, 'is it so very surprising if it remains in this world for a time?'

3

Suddenly the telephone on his desk began to ring. Usually it made a very loud, demanding sound. This time it was ringing very softly. 'Perhaps there is something wrong with it,' thought Teesdale. However, the telephone was certainly ringing, and he got up and picked up the receiver.

'Hullo,' he said.

All he could hear was a whisper. 'I can't hear you,' he said. 'Speak louder, please!'

Again the whisper came, but Teesdale could not hear a word of it. Then it became softer, and died away.

He stood there for a few moments. Then he telephoned the operator. 'I've just had a telephone call,' he said. 'Can you tell me where the call came from, please?'

The operator checked, and gave him a number. To Teesdale's surprise it was the number of the prison. He at once telephoned them.

The voice on the telephone was clear and strong. Teesdale recognized the voice of Prison Officer Draycott. 'There must be some mistake, Doctor. We haven't telephoned you.'

'But the operator says you did, about five minutes ago.'

'The operator must be mistaken, Doctor. Sorry.'

'Very strange. Well, good night, Draycott.'

Teesdale sat down again. 'What a very strange thing,' he said to himself. He thought about the soft ringing of the telephone bell, and the quiet whisper when he answered it. 'I wonder . . .' he said. 'No – no, it's impossible.'

Next morning he went to the prison as usual. Once again

he was conscious of an unseen presence near him. He felt it most strongly in the prison yard, near the hanging-shed. At the same time he was conscious of a deep and mysterious horror deep inside him. The spirit needed help. This feeling was so strong there that he almost expected to see Linkworth standing there, watching him.

He went back to the prison hospital and concentrated on his work. But the feeling of an unseen presence never left him. Finally, before he went home, Teesdale looked into the hanging-shed. At the top of the steps stood the condemned man with the rope around his neck. Teesdale turned in horror and came out at once, his face grey with fear. He was a brave man and he was soon ashamed of his fear. He decided to go back into the shed, but his muscles would not obey the orders of his mind. Suddenly Teesdale had an idea. He sent for Prison Officer Draycott.

'Are you quite sure,' he said, 'that nobody telephoned me last night?'

Draycott hesitated for a moment. 'I don't think anybody telephoned, Doctor. I was sitting near the telephone. If anybody used it, why didn't I see them?'

'You *saw* nobody,' said the doctor.

'That's right, sir . . .' He hesitated again.

'Did you perhaps have the feeling that there was someone there?' asked the doctor gently.

'Well, yes, sir,' said Draycott. 'But I expect I was wrong. Perhaps I was half asleep. I expect I made a mistake.'

'And perhaps you did not!' said the doctor. 'I know that I didn't make a mistake when I heard my telephone ringing last night. It didn't ring in its usual way. The sound was so soft that I could only just hear it. And when I picked it up, I could only hear a whisper. But when I talked to you, your voice was loud and clear. Now I believe that someone – something – telephoned me last night. You were there, and you felt their presence, although you could not see anything.'

Draycott said, 'I'm not a nervous man, Doctor. I haven't much imagination. But there *was* something there. It was a warm night, and there was no wind. But something moved the pages of the telephone book. It blew on my face. And it was bitterly cold, sir.'

The doctor looked seriously at him. 'Did it remind you of anything, or anybody? Did a name come into your mind?' he asked.

'Yes, sir. Linkworth, sir,' said Draycott at once.

'Are you on duty tonight?' asked the doctor.

'Yes, Doctor – and I wish I wasn't!'

'I know how you feel. Now, listen. I am sure this – this thing wants to communicate with me. Give it a chance to get to the telephone. Stay away from the telephone for an hour, between half past nine and half past ten this evening. I'll wait for the call. And if I do receive a call, I'll telephone you at once.'

'And there is nothing to be afraid of?' said Draycott anxiously.

'I'm sure there's nothing to be afraid of,' said the doctor gently.

4

At half past nine Teesdale was sitting in his study. 'If it telephones,' he thought, 'I think it will telephone at the same time as last night.' Just then the telephone rang, not as softly as before, but still more quietly than usual.

Teesdale picked up the receiver and held it to his ear. Someone was crying. It was a heartbroken, hopeless sound. He listened for a moment, then he spoke.

'Yes, yes,' he said kindly. 'This is Doctor Teesdale speaking. What can I do for you? And where are you speaking from?' He did not say, 'Who are you?' – he was sure he knew the answer.

Slowly the crying stopped, and a soft voice whispered, 'I want to tell, sir – I want to tell – I must tell.'

'Yes, you can tell me,' said the doctor.

'I can't tell you, sir. There's another gentleman, sir. He used to come to see me in the prison. Will you give him a message, sir? I can't make him hear me, or see me. Tell him it's Linkworth, sir. Charles Linkworth. I'm very miserable. I can't leave the prison – and it's so cold. Will you send for the other gentleman?'

'Do you mean the chaplain?' asked Teesdale.

'Yes, that's right – the chaplain. He was there when I went across the yard yesterday. He prayed for me. I'll feel better when I've told him, sir.'

The doctor hesitated for a moment. 'This is a strange story,' he thought. 'How can I possibly tell the chaplain that the spirit of a dead man is trying to telephone him?' But

Teesdale himself believed that the unhappy spirit wanted to confess. And there was no need to ask *what* it wanted to confess . . . 'Yes,' said Teesdale aloud, 'I'll ask him to come here.'

'Thank you, sir, a thousand times,' said the voice. It was growing softer. 'I can't talk any more now. I have to go to see – oh, my God . . .' The terrible, desperate crying began again.

'What do you have to see?' asked Teesdale with sudden, desperate curiosity. 'Tell me what you are doing – tell me what's happening to you.'

'I can't tell you; I'm not allowed to tell you,' said the voice very softly. 'That is part . . .' and the voice died away.

Doctor Teesdale waited a little while, but no more sounds came from the receiver. He put it down. His forehead was wet with the cold sweat of horror, and his heart was beating very fast. 'Is this real?' he asked himself, 'or is it some terrible joke?' But in his heart he knew that he had been speaking to a troubled spirit, a spirit that had something terrible to confess.

He telephoned the prison. 'Draycott?' he asked. The prison officer's voice trembled as he answered. 'Yes, sir.'

'Has anything happened, Draycott?'

Twice the man attempted to speak, and twice he failed. At last the words came. 'Yes, sir. He has been here. I saw him go into the room where the telephone is.'

'Ah! Did you speak to him?'

'No, sir. I sweated and I prayed.'

'Well, I don't think you will be disturbed again. Now please give me the chaplain's home address.'

5

The next evening the two gentlemen had dinner together in the doctor's dining-room. When Mrs Parker had left them with their coffee and cigarettes, Teesdale spoke to the chaplain. 'My dear Dawkins,' he said, 'You will think this is very strange. But last night and the night before, I spoke on the telephone with the spirit of Charles Linkworth.'

'The man they hanged two days ago?' said Dawkins. 'Really, Teesdale, if you've brought me here to tell ghost stories . . .'

'He asked me to bring you here, Dawkins. He wants to tell you something. I think you can guess what it is.'

'I don't want to know,' said the chaplain angrily. 'Dead men do not return. They have finished with this world; they don't come back.'

'But listen,' said Teesdale. 'Two nights ago my telephone rang, but very softly, and I could only hear whispers. I asked the operator where the call came from. It came from the prison. I telephoned the prison, and Prison Officer Draycott told me that nobody had telephoned from there. But he was conscious of a presence in the room.'

'That man drinks too much whisky,' said the chaplain sharply.

'He's a good officer,' said Teesdale, 'and very sensible. And anyway, *I* do not drink whisky!'

Suddenly the telephone in the study rang. The doctor heard it clearly. 'There!' he said. 'Can't you hear it?'

'I can't hear anything,' said the chaplain angrily.

The doctor got up and went to the telephone. 'Yes?' he said in a trembling voice. 'Who is it? Yes, Mr Dawkins is here. I'll try to get him to speak to you.'

He went back into the dining-room. 'Dawkins,' he said, 'Please listen to him. I beg you to listen to him.'

The chaplain hesitated a moment. 'Very well,' he said at last. He went to the telephone and held the receiver to his ear.

'I can't hear anything,' he said. 'Ah – I heard something there. A very soft whisper.'

'Try to hear!' begged the doctor.

Again the chaplain listened. Suddenly he put the receiver down. He frowned. 'Something – somebody said, "I killed her. I confess. I want to be forgiven." It's a joke, my dear Teesdale. Somebody is playing a sick, horrible joke on you. I *can't* believe it.'

Doctor Teesdale picked up the receiver. 'Teesdale here,' he said. 'Can you give Mr Dawkins a sign that you are there?' He put the receiver down again. 'He says he thinks he can,' he said. 'We must wait.'

It was a warm evening and the window was open. For five minutes the two men sat and waited, but nothing happened. Then the chaplain spoke. 'There!' he said, 'Nothing at all! I think that proves I'm right.'

As he spoke an icy wind suddenly blew into the room. It moved the papers on the doctor's desk. Teesdale went to the window and closed it.

'Did you feel that?' he asked.

'Yes,' said the chaplain. 'A breath of cold air from the window.'

57

Once again the cold wind blew in the closed room. 'And did you feel that?' asked the doctor gently.

The chaplain's hands trembled. 'Dear God,' he prayed, 'keep us safe this night.'

'Something is coming!' said the doctor. And it came. In the centre of the room stood the figure of a man. His head was bent over onto his shoulder, and they could not see his face. Then he took his head in both hands and raised it slowly and heavily. The dead face looked at them. The mouth was open; the dead eyes stared. There was a red line around the neck. Then there came the sound of something falling on the floor. The figure disappeared. But on the carpet of the study lay a rope.

For a long time nobody spoke. The sweat poured off the doctor's face. The chaplain was whispering prayers through pale lips. The doctor pointed at the rope.

'That rope has been missing since Linkworth was hanged,' he said.

Then again the telephone rang. This time the chaplain picked up the receiver at once. He listened in silence.

'Charles Linkworth,' he said at last, 'are you truly sorry for your crime?' He waited for an answer, then he whispered the words of forgiveness.

'I can't hear any more,' said the chaplain, replacing the receiver.

Just then Parker came in with more coffee. Doctor Teesdale pointed to the place where the ghost had stood. 'Take that rope, Parker, and burn it,' he said.

There was a moment's silence.

'There is no rope, sir,' said Parker.

The mouth was open; the dead eyes stared.

The Ghost Coach

1

This is a true story. Although twenty years have passed since that night, I can still remember everything about it very clearly indeed. During those twenty years I have told the story to only one other person. I still feel uncomfortable about telling it. Be patient with me, please. Do not argue, and do not try to explain anything. I do not want your explanations. I do not welcome your arguments. I was there, after all, and I have had twenty years to think about it.

I had been shooting in the lonely hills in the north of England. I had been out all day with my gun, but without success. It was December and a bitterly cold east wind was blowing. Snow was beginning to fall from a heavy grey sky. It was becoming dark and I realized that I had lost my way. I looked around me, and saw no signs of human life.

'Oh well!' I thought, 'I must just keep on walking, and perhaps I'll find shelter somewhere.' I put my gun under my arm and started walking.

The snow fell heavily. It became very cold, and night was falling fast. I was very tired and hungry. I had been out all day and I had eaten nothing since breakfast. I thought about my young wife in the hotel in the village.

'How worried she will be!' I thought. 'I promised to come back before nightfall. I wish I could keep that promise!'

We had been married just four months. We loved each

other very much, and of course we were very happy together. I hated to worry her.

'Well,' I thought. 'Perhaps I'll find shelter somewhere. Perhaps I'll meet someone who can tell me how to get back to the hotel. Then with luck I'll see my dear wife before midnight.'

All the time the snow was falling and the night was becoming darker. Every few steps I stopped and shouted, but the only sound in that wild, lonely place was the wind. I began to feel uneasy. I had read stories about travellers who were lost in the snow. They walked until they were too tired to walk any more. Then they lay down in the snow, and fell asleep, and never woke up again.

'That mustn't happen to me!' I said to myself. 'I can't let it happen! I mustn't die, when I have so much to live for! What would my poor wife do without me?' I pushed away these frightening ideas. I shouted louder, and then listened for an answer. Above the sad, complaining sounds of the wind I thought I heard a far-off cry. I shouted again, and again I imagined that I heard an answer. Then out of the darkness appeared a little white circle of light. It came nearer; it became brighter. I ran towards it as fast as I could – and found an old man with a lantern.

'Thank God!' I cried. I was very, very pleased to see him.

He did not look at all glad to see me, however. He lifted his lantern and stared into my face.

'What are you thanking God for?' he growled.

'Well – I was thanking Him for you. I was afraid that I was lost in the snow.'

'Where are you trying to get to?'

'Dwolding. How far is it from here?' I asked.

'About twenty miles,' the old man growled. 'So you *are* lost, after all.'

'Oh dear. And where is the nearest village?'

'The nearest village is Wyke, and that's twelve miles away from here.'

'Where do you live, then?'

'Over there,' he said, pointing with the lantern.

'Are you going home, then?' I asked.

'Perhaps I am.'

'Then please let me go home with you,' I said.

The old man shook his head. 'That's no good,' he said. 'He won't let you in.'

'Oh, I'm sure he will,' I said. 'Who is "he"?'

'My master.'

'Who is your master?' I asked.

'That's none of your business,' was the old man's rude reply.

'Well, please take me to him. I'm sure that your master will give me shelter and supper tonight.'

'Well, I don't think he will, but I suppose you can always ask!' the old man said crossly. He shook his grey head again and started walking. I followed the light of his lantern through the falling snow. Suddenly I saw a big black shape in the darkness. A huge dog came running towards me. It growled angrily.

'Down, King!' said the old man.

'Is this the house?' I asked.

'Yes, this is the house . . . Down, King!' And he took a key out of his pocket.

The door was huge and heavy. It looked like the door of a prison. The old man turned the key and I saw my chance. Quickly I pushed past him into the house.

2

I looked around me. I was in a very big, high hall. While I was looking, a bell rang loudly.

'That's for you,' said the old man. He gave an unfriendly smile. 'That's the master's room, over there.'

He pointed to a low black door at the opposite side of the hall. I walked up to it and knocked loudly. Then I went in without waiting for an invitation. An old man with white hair was sitting at a table. Papers and books covered the table. He got up and looked very hard at me.

'Who are you?' he said. 'How did you get here, and what do you want?'

'My name is James Murray,' I answered. 'I'm a doctor. I walked here across the hills. I need food, drink and sleep.'

'This is not a hotel!' he said. 'Jacob, why did you let this stranger into my house?'

'I didn't let him in,' growled the old man. 'He followed me home, and he pushed past me into the house. I couldn't stop him. He's bigger than I am!'

His employer turned to me. 'And why did you do that, sir?' he asked.

'To save my life,' I answered at once.

'To save your life?'

63

'The snow is deep already,' I replied. 'It will be deep enough to bury me before morning!'

He walked over to the window and looked out at the falling snow. 'It's true,' he said at last. 'You may stay until morning, if you wish. Jacob, bring our supper . . . Sit down, please.'

He sat down at the table again and began to read.

I put my gun in a corner. I sat down near the fire and looked around me. This room was smaller than the hall, but I could see many unusual and interesting things in it. There were books on every chair. There were maps and papers on the floor. 'What an interesting room!' I said to myself. 'And what a strange place to live! Here, in this lonely farmhouse, among these dark hills!' I looked round the room, then I looked again at the old man. I wondered about him. 'Who is he?' I thought. 'What is he?' He had a big, beautiful head. It was covered with thick white hair. He had a strong, clever, serious face. There were lines of concentration across his wide, high forehead, and lines of sadness around his mouth.

Jacob brought in our supper. His master closed his book and invited me politely to the table.

There was a large plate with meat, brown bread and eggs, and a pot of good, strong coffee.

'I hope you're hungry, sir,' said the old man. 'I have nothing better to offer you.'

But my mouth was already full of bread and meat. 'It's excellent,' I said gratefully. 'Thank you very much.'

'You're welcome,' he said politely but coldly. His supper, I saw, was only bread and milk. We ate without speaking. The old man seemed sad. I tried to imagine why he lived such a quiet and lonely life in this far-off place.

When we had finished, Jacob took the empty plates away. His master got up and looked out of the window.

'It has stopped snowing,' he said.

I jumped up. 'Stopped snowing!' I cried. 'Then perhaps – No, of course I can't. I can't walk twenty miles tonight.'

'Walk twenty miles!' repeated the old man in surprise. 'What do you mean?'

'My wife is waiting for me,' I said. 'She does not know where I am. I'm sure she's very worried.'

'Where is she?'

'At Dwolding, twenty miles away.'

'At Dwolding,' he said slowly. 'Yes, that's right; it *is* twenty miles away. But do you have to go there at once?'

'Oh yes,' I answered. 'She'll be desperate with worry. I'll do anything . . .'

'Well,' said the old man after a moment's hesitation. 'There is a coach. It goes along the old coach road every night, and it always stops at Dwolding.' He looked at the clock on the wall. 'In about an hour and a quarter, the coach should stop at a signpost about five miles from here. Jacob can go with you, and show you the old coach road that leads to the signpost. If he does that, do you think you'll be able to find the signpost all right?'

'Easily – and thank you.'

He smiled for the first time, and rang the bell. He gave Jacob his orders, then turned to me. 'You must hurry,' he said, 'if you want to catch the coach. Good night!'

I thanked him warmly. I wanted to shake his hand, but he had already turned away.

3

Soon Jacob and I were out on the lonely, snow-covered hills. Although the wind was quieter, it was still bitterly cold. The sky was starless. The only noise in that wild, empty place was the sound of our footsteps in the snow. Jacob did not speak. He walked silently along in front of me, holding the lantern. I followed, with my gun under my arm. I was silent too, because I was thinking about the old man. I could still hear his voice. I remembered every word of our conversation; in fact, I can still remember it today.

Suddenly Jacob stopped, and pointed with the lantern. 'That's your road. Keep that stone wall on your right and you can't go wrong.'

'This is the old coach road, then?' I asked him.

'That's right,' he growled.

'And how far am I from the signpost?'

'About three miles. Just follow the road. You can't miss it.'

I took out my wallet, and he became more helpful. 'It's a good road,' he said, 'for walkers; but it was too steep and narrow for coaches. Be careful – the wall is broken, near the signpost. It was never mended after the accident.'

'What accident?'

'The night coach went off the road. It fell over the edge of the road and down into the valley. It's a long way down – fifty feet or more. It's a very bad piece of road just there.'

'How terrible!' I cried. 'Were many people killed?'

'They were all killed. Four passengers were found dead, and the driver died the next morning.'

'How long ago did this happen?'

'Twenty years. My master has been a broken man since that day. His only son was one of the passengers. That's why he shuts himself away in that lonely place.'

'The wall is broken near the signpost? Thank you. I'll remember that. Good night.' I pushed a silver coin into his hand.

'Good night, sir, and thank you,' said Jacob. He turned and walked away.

I watched the light of his lantern until it disappeared. Then I began to walk along the old coach road.

This was not difficult. Although it was dark, I could still see the stone wall at the edge of the road. 'I'm safe,' I told myself. But I felt very lonely and a little afraid. I tried to forget my loneliness and fear. I sang and I whistled. I thought about my dear wife, and for a short time I felt better.

But the night was very cold. Although I walked quickly, I was unable to keep warm. My hands and feet were like ice. My chest felt icy cold and I had difficulty in breathing. My gun seemed terribly heavy. I was very tired and began to feel ill. I had to stop and rest for a moment. Just then I saw a circle of light, a long way away, like the light of a lantern. At first I thought that Jacob had come back again, to make sure I was all right. Then I saw a second light beside the first. I realized that they were the two lights of a coach.

'But how strange,' I thought, 'to use this dangerous old road. Jacob said nobody had used it since that terrible accident.' Then I thought again. 'Have I walked past the signpost in the dark? Is this the night coach that goes to Dwolding, after all?'

Meanwhile the coach came along the road. It was moving very fast, and noiselessly over the snowy road. I saw the huge dark shape of the coach with its driver on top and its four fine grey horses.

I jumped forward and shouted and waved. The coach went past me, and for a moment I thought it was not going to stop. But it did stop. The driver did not look at me. The guard seemed to be asleep. Everyone was silent and still. I ran up to the coach. Nobody moved to help me. I had to open the door of the coach for myself with my stiff, frozen fingers. 'It's empty,' I thought.

But there were three travellers in the coach. None of them moved or looked at me. They all seemed asleep. I got in and sat down. The inside of the coach seemed very cold . . . even colder than outside. The air inside the coach smelt heavy, damp and . . . dead. I looked around at the other passengers and tried to start a conversation.

'It's very cold tonight,' I said politely to the passenger who was sitting opposite me.

He turned his head towards me slowly, but did not answer.

'I think winter is really here,' I continued. The passenger was sitting in a dark corner and I could not see his face. But I could see his eyes. He was looking straight at me, but still he did not say a word.

'Why doesn't he answer?' I thought. But I did not feel really angry. I was too tired and too cold for that. I was still stiff with cold and tiredness, and the strange, damp smell inside the coach was making me feel sick too. I was frozen to my bones, and trembling with cold. I turned to the passenger on my left.

'May I open the window?' I asked politely.

He did not speak. He did not move.

I repeated my question more loudly, but he still did not answer. Then I became impatient. I tried to open the window – and I saw the glass. It was covered with dirt. 'My God – they haven't cleaned this glass for years!' I said to myself. I looked around the coach, and suddenly I thought I understood the reason for the strange smell. Everything was dirty, old and damp. The floor was almost breaking away under my feet. I turned to the third passenger.

'This coach is falling to pieces,' I said to him. 'I expect the coach company are using this one while the usual coach is being repaired.'

He moved his head slowly and still looked at me in silence. I shall never forget that look. I can still remember it now . . . His eyes burned with a wild, unnatural light. His face was greenish white. 'Like a dead man,' I said to myself. Then I saw that his bloodless lips were pulled back from his huge white teeth . . . I trembled with fear and horror. Then I looked again at the passenger opposite me. He too was staring at me. His face was deathly white, and his eyes shone with an unearthly light. I looked again at the passenger on my left. I saw – oh, how can I describe him? I saw the face of a dead man. All three passengers were dead. A greenish light shone from their terrible faces. Their damp hair smelt of death. Their clothes smelt of the graveyard. I

69

knew then that their bodies were dead. Only their terrible, shining eyes were alive – and they were all staring at me, threatening me.

I gave a scream of horror. I had to get out of that terrible place. I threw myself at the door and tried desperately to open it. Just then the moon came out from behind a cloud. In its cool, silvery light I suddenly saw everything very clearly. I saw the signpost pointing along the road like a warning finger. I saw the broken wall at the edge of the road. I saw the frightened horses on the edge of a steep drop. I saw the valley fifty feet below us. The coach shook like a ship at sea. There were screams of men and of horses. There was a tearing crash, a moment of terrible pain, and then – darkness.

4

A very long time later I woke from a deep sleep. I found my wife sitting by my bed. 'What . . . what happened?' I asked.

'You fell, dear,' she said. 'The wall was broken at the edge of the road, and you fell down into the valley. It was fifty feet, dear – but you were lucky. There was a lot of deep snow at the bottom, and that saved your life.'

'I can't remember anything. How did I get here?'

'Two farm workers were out early in the morning, looking for their lost sheep. They found you in the snow and they carried you to the nearest shelter. They fetched a doctor. You were very ill. Your arm was broken, and you

*I saw the frightened horses and the coach on the
edge of a steep drop.*

had had a terrible bang on the head. You were unconscious and couldn't tell them anything. But the doctor looked in your pockets and found your name and address. So of course he called me, my dearest. And I've been looking after you since then. Now you mustn't worry. You must rest, and concentrate on getting well again.'

I was young and healthy and I was soon out of danger. But while I lay in my bed I thought about the accident. Perhaps you can guess exactly where I fell that night. It was the place where the coach had gone off the road twenty years before.

I never told my wife this story. I told the doctor; but he said that the whole adventure was just a dream, the result of cold, tiredness and a violent bang on the head. I tried to make him understand, but he refused to listen to me. I did not argue; it did not really matter if he believed me or not. But I knew then, and I know now. Twenty years ago I was a passenger in a Ghost Coach.

Fullcircle

1

One late afternoon in October Leithen and I climbed the hill above the stream and came in sight of the house. It had been a beautiful, misty morning, but now the mist had cleared. The warm sunshine of autumn shone on the fields, and on the trees the leaves were red and gold. We were looking down into a little valley like a green cup in the hills. It was a beautiful place. There was an old stone wall, and a little wood. Then there was smooth green grass, and a tiny lake. And at the heart of it all, like a jewel in a ring, stood the house. It was very small, but everything about it was quite perfect. It was old – perhaps seventeenth century – with large, light windows and pale stone walls.

Leithen looked at me. 'Isn't it fine?' he said to me. 'It was built by the great Sir Christopher Wren. You know – the man who built St Paul's Cathedral in London. The house has a most unusual name too. It is called Fullcircle. Don't you think that name suits it rather well?'

He told me the story of the house. 'It was built about 1660 by Lord Carteron. He didn't like the bright lights of the city. He was a sensitive and well-educated man and wrote some fine books in English and Latin. He loved beautiful things, and he employed the best builders and gardeners in England to work on Fullcircle. The result was a wonderful success for Wren, for the garden planners and for Carteron himself – a triumph, in fact. When the house was finished, he hid himself away for months at a time, with only a few good friends and his beloved books and garden. Rather a selfish man, really. He didn't do much for his king or his country. But he certainly had style. He knew how to enjoy life. He knew how to live well. He did only one foolish thing in his whole life. He became a Catholic. That was a dangerous thing to do in those days. Catholics were not popular then. Fortunately nobody punished him for it.'

'What happened to the house after Lord Carteron died?' I asked.

'He had no children, so some cousins moved into the house. Then in the eighteenth century the Applebys bought Fullcircle. They were country gentlemen, and very fond of hunting and shooting. They didn't take very good care of the library. But they enjoyed life too, in their own way. Old John Appleby was a friend of mine. Something went wrong with his stomach when he was about seventy. The doctor decided to forbid him to drink whisky. Poor old John, he had never drunk really heavily, although he always enjoyed a drink. "Do you know, Leithen," he told me. "Since I stopped drinking whisky I've realized something. I've lived a long life – a useful one too, I hope. But in all that time I've never been completely sober." Anyway, he died last year. He was a good old man, and I still miss him. The house went to a distant cousin called Giffen.'

He laughed. 'Julian and Ursula Giffen . . . perhaps you've heard of them. People like the Giffens always go about in pairs. They write books about society and personal relationships – books called 'The New Something', or 'Towards Something Else', or 'An Examination of Something

Completely Different'. You know the sort of thing . . . Good, kind people, but extraordinarily silly. I first met them at a trial. The criminal was certainly guilty, but the police couldn't prove it. The Giffens were involved, of course. They felt sorry for the poor criminal . . . Well, I went two or three times to their house in north London. Dear God! What a place! No comfortable chairs, and the ugliest curtains I've ever seen. No style, you see. They didn't know how to live well.'

'I'm surprised that you are so friendly with them,' I said. 'They don't sound your kind of couple at all.'

'Oh, I like human beings. Lawyers like me have to study people; it's part of our job. And really the Giffens have hearts of gold. They are sensitive and kind, and somehow very innocent. They know so little about life . . . I wonder how they will like living in Fullcircle.'

2

Just then we heard the sound of bicycle wheels on the road. The rider saw Leithen and got off his bike. He was quite tall, perhaps forty years old. A big brown beard covered the lower half of his thin, pale, serious face. Thick glasses covered his short-sighted eyes. He wore short brown trousers and a rather ugly green shirt.

'This is Julian Giffen,' said Leithen to me. 'Julian, this is Harry Peck. He's staying with me. We stopped to look at your house. Could we possibly have a quick look inside? I want Peck to see the staircase.'

'Of course,' said Mr Giffen. 'I've just been into the village to post a letter. I hope you'll stay to tea. Some very interesting people are coming for the weekend.'

He was gentle and polite, and clearly he loved talking. He led us through a gate and into a perfect little rose garden. Then we stood in front of the doorway, with *Carpe Diem* above the door. I have never seen anything like that hall, with its lovely curving staircase. It was small, but every detail was perfect. It seemed full of sunlight, and it had an air of peace, confidence and happiness.

Giffen led us into a room on the left. 'You remember the house in Mr Appleby's time, don't you, Leithen? This was the chapel. We've made a few changes . . . Excuse me, Mr Peck, you aren't a Catholic, are you?'

It was a beautiful little room. It had the same look of sunny cheerfulness as the rest of the house. But there were new wooden shelves against the walls. They were covered with ugly new paperback books and piles of papers. A big table with a green tablecloth filled most of the floor. Two typewriters stood on a side-table.

'This is our workroom,' explained Giffen. 'We hold our Sunday meetings here. Ursula thinks that every weekend we ought to produce some really useful work. We welcome busy people to our home, and we give them a pleasant place to work in.'

A woman came into the room. 'She could be pretty,' I said to myself, 'if she tried.' But she did not try. She had tied back her reddish hair behind her ears. Her clothes were ugly, and wildly unsuitable for a country life. She had bright, eager eyes like a bird, and her hands trembled nervously. She greeted Leithen warmly.

'We're so comfortable here,' she said. 'Julian and I feel as if we've always lived here. Our life has arranged itself so perfectly. My Home for Unmarried Mothers in the village will soon be ready. I plan to bring young women from London to it. Our Workers' Education Classes will open in the winter . . . And it's so nice to invite our friends here . . . Won't you stay to tea? Doctor Swope is coming, and Mary Elliston, from the New Society Group. And Mr Percy Blaker, from Free Thought Magazine. I'm sure you'll enjoy meeting them . . . Must you hurry away? I'm so sorry . . . What do you think of our workroom? It was horrible when we arrived here – a kind of chapel, rather dark and mysterious. It's so much lighter and brighter now.'

'Yes,' I remarked politely. 'The whole house looks beautifully light and bright.'

'Ah, you've noticed. It's a strangely happy place to live in. It's just right for us, of course. It's so easy to influence it, to change it to suit our way of life.'

We said goodbye. We did not wish to meet Doctor Swope or Mary Elliston, or Mr Percy Blaker. When we reached the road we stopped and looked down again at the little house. The setting sun had turned the pale stone walls to gold. It looked very calm and peaceful. I thought about the good-hearted couple inside its walls, and suddenly they seemed unimportant. They just did not matter. The house was the important thing. It had a masterful look; it seemed timeless, ageless, confident in its beauty. 'Mrs Giffen won't find it easy to influence this house,' I said to myself. 'It's much more likely to influence her!'

That night in the library of his house, Leithen talked about the seventeenth century. 'The previous century was full of darkness and mystery and fear. The people knew all about pain and death; they lived with pain and death every day, and they faced them bravely. They had their happy times, of course, but they had their dark, desperate ones too. Their lives were like our weather – storm and sun. After 1660 things were different, calmer, less troubled. Those people knew how to live. Look at Fullcircle. There are no dark corners there. The man who built it understood how to find calm, gentle enjoyment in life . . . The trouble was, he was afraid of death. So he joined the Catholic church, just to make sure . . .'

3

Two years later I saw the Giffens again. It was almost the end of the fishing season. I had taken a day off from my work, and I was doing a little gentle fishing in a river near Leithen's house. Another man was fishing from the opposite bank. It was Giffen. I stood watching while he caught a large fish. Later I called to him, and we ate our sandwiches together. He had changed a lot. He had shaved off his beard, and his face looked less thin and less serious than before. He was sunburnt too, and looked more like a countryman than before. His clothes, too, were different.

They were good, sensible, country clothes, and suited him well.

'I didn't know you were a fisherman,' I said to him.

'Oh, yes,' he said. 'I love it. This is only my second season of fishing and I'm learning all the time. I wish I'd started years ago. I never realized what good fun fishing was. Isn't this a beautiful place?'

'I'm glad you enjoy fishing,' I said. 'It will help you to enjoy your weekends in the country.'

'Oh, we don't go to London much these days,' he answered. 'We sold our London house a year ago. We never felt at home in London, somehow. We are both so happy here. It's nice to see things growing.'

I liked him. He was beginning to talk like a true countryman.

After a good day's fishing he persuaded me to spend the night at Fullcircle. 'You can catch the early train tomorrow morning,' he said. He drove me there in his little green car ('What has happened to his bicycle?' I wondered) along four miles of country road, with the birds singing in every tree.

Dinner was my first big surprise. It was simple, but perfectly cooked, with wonderful fresh vegetables. There was some excellent wine too. 'Strange,' I thought. 'I'm sure the Giffens are the authors of "Stay Sober, Stay Healthy".'

My second surprise was Mrs Giffen herself. Her clothes were pretty and sensible, and they suited her perfectly. But the real difference was in her face. I suddenly realized that she was a pretty woman. Her face seemed softer and rounder. She looked calm and happy, and pleased with her life.

I asked about her Home for Unmarried Mothers. She laughed cheerfully. 'I closed it after the first year. The mothers didn't feel comfortable with the people in the village. Londoners don't like the country – it's too quiet for them, I suppose. Julian and I have decided that our business is to look after our own people here in the country.'

Perhaps it was unkind of me, but I mentioned the Workers' Education Classes. Giffen looked a little ashamed. 'I stopped it because I didn't think it was doing any good. Why give people things that they don't need? Education is a wonderful thing. But education, like medicine, is only useful when a person needs it, and the people here don't need it. They can teach me so much about the important things in life – I don't have anything so important to teach them.'

'Anyway, dear,' said his wife, 'you're so busy, with the house and the garden and the farm. It isn't a large place, but it takes up a lot of your time.'

I noticed a picture on the dining-room wall. It showed a middle-aged man in the clothes of the late seventeenth-century. He had a sensitive, intelligent face.

'That's an interesting picture,' I said to Giffen.

'That's Lord Carteron,' he said. 'He built this house. We've fallen in love with Fullcircle, you see. We wanted a picture of its builder. I found this one at a big sale in London, and I had to pay a lot of money for it. It's a nice picture to live with.'

He was right. It was a most pleasing picture. The face in the picture looked confident and sensible. It was a kind face, but it had a rather masterful look about it. 'A good friend,' I thought, 'and an amusing companion.'

Giffen saw me looking, and smiled. 'I like having him in the house,' he said.

We moved into the room beside the hall. Two years before, it had been the Giffens' workroom. Now, I saw with surprise, it was a kind of smoking-room. There were comfortable leather chairs and beautiful old wooden bookshelves. On the wall were pictures of people hunting and fishing. Above the fireplace was a stag's head.

'I shot him last year in Scotland,' said Giffen triumphantly. 'My first stag.'

That surprised me. So Julian Giffen enjoyed hunting as well as fishing. It was very unexpected.

On a little table were copies of *The Field*, *Country Life* and other magazines. Nothing educational at all. Giffen saw the surprise on my face.

'We get these magazines for our guests,' he said. ('And who are the guests? Not Doctor Swope and his companions, surely!' I said to myself with a secret smile.)

I have many faults; and one of them is looking at other people's books. I examined the books in the Giffens' bookshelves, and was pleasantly surprised. All my old favourites were there. There was nothing about 'The New Something', or 'Towards Something Else', or 'An Examination of Something Completely Different'.

As I sat in my comfortable chair I had a very strange feeling. It seemed to me that I was watching a play. The Giffens were the actors, and they were moving quite happily about the stage in obedience to some unseen stage-manager. Then, as I looked, the actors and the stage seemed to disappear. I was conscious of only one 'person' – the house itself. It sat there in its little valley, smiling at all our modern ideas. And all the time its spirit worked its gentle influence on those who loved it. The house was more than a building; it was an art, a way of life. Its spirit was older than Carteron, older than England. A long time ago, in ancient Greece and Rome, there were places like Fullcircle. But in those days they were called temples, and gods lived in them.

But Giffen was talking about his books. 'I've been relearning my Latin and Greek,' he said. 'I haven't looked at them since I left university. And there are so many good English books too, that I haven't read yet. I wish I had more time for reading; it means a lot to me.'

'There are so many lovely things to do here,' said his wife. 'The days are too short. It's lovely to be busy, doing things that I really enjoy.'

'All the same,' said Giffen, 'I wish I could do more reading. I never wanted to before.'

'But you come in tired from your shooting, and then you sleep until dinner,' said his wife lovingly.

They were happy people, and I like happiness. 'They know how to enjoy life,' I thought. Then I had a feeling of uneasiness. 'They have changed so quickly,' I thought. 'Too quickly. Something or someone has influenced them. They are nicer, pleasanter people now. But are they free? Are they doing what *they* want to do? Or are they just actors on a stage?'

As Mrs Giffen showed me up to my room, she smiled and said, 'Isn't it wonderful? We've found the perfect house for us. It's been so easy to change it to suit our way of life.'

I looked at her, and I wondered again who was doing the changing.

At the heart of it all, like a jewel in a ring, stood the house.

4

One November afternoon Leithen and I were coming home from a ride. We were cold and wet and very tired.

'Let's look in at Fullcircle,' said Leithen. 'It isn't far, and the Giffens will give us tea. You'll find a few changes there.'

'What changes?' I asked.

'Wait and see,' said Leithen with a smile.

I wondered about these changes as we rode towards the house. Nothing bad, surely; the little house would never allow it.

The house was lovelier than ever. Outside it was a dark November day, but the house seemed full of sunshine. A bright fire burned in the fireplace. There was a smell of wood smoke and flowers, and the house felt as warm and as kind as summer.

We sat by the dining-room fire drinking our hot tea. I looked around for the changes that Leithen had mentioned. I did not find them in Giffen. He was exactly as I remembered him, that June night after our fishing. He looked like an intelligent, sensitive man, completely happy with his life. Was it my imagination, or did he look a little like the picture of Lord Carteron? I looked at him, and then at the picture. 'Yes,' I thought. 'There is something there.'

But his wife! Ah, the change was unmistakable. She was a little fatter, a little rounder. There were rings on her pretty hands. She talked more and laughed more often.

'We're going to give a dance at Christmas,' she said.

84

'Promise me you'll come. We must do something to make the country cheerful in wintertime.'

'To me,' I said, 'Fullcircle seems cheerful all through the year.'

'How kind of you to say that!' she said. 'If you say nice things about our house, you're really saying them about us too. A house is just what its owners make of it.'

I was filling my pipe in the hall. I was just going to take it into the smoking-room when Giffen stopped me.

'We don't smoke there now,' he said. He opened the door and I looked in. The bookshelves had disappeared. It looked like a church. There was a little altar at one end of the room, and a big silver cross. A silver lamp burned on the altar.

Giffen shut the door quietly. 'Perhaps you didn't know. Some months ago my wife became a Catholic. So we made this room into a chapel again. It always *was* a chapel, of course, in the days of the Carterons and the Applebys.'

'And you?' I asked.

'I don't think much about these things. But I'll do the same soon. It will please Ursula if we pray together. And it can't harm anybody.'

5

Leithen and I stopped at the top of the hill and looked down again into the little green valley. Leithen laughed softly. 'That house!' he said. 'I'm going to read everything I can find about old Carteron. I'm sure he was an extraordinarily clever man. I'm sure his spirit is still alive down there. He's making other people do as he did. You can send away the chaplain, and turn the house upside-down. But Carteron will get what he wants in the end.'

The sun came out from behind a cloud, and shone on the stone walls of Fullcircle. It seemed to me that the house had a look of gentle triumph.

GLOSSARY

admit to say or agree that you did something wrong

alarm *(n)* a warning sound (e.g. a bell) when there is danger

altar the table at the end of a church, usually with a cross on it

Bible the holy book of the Christian church

blank *(adj)* without any writing or drawing

carpe diem an expression in Latin which means 'Enjoy today'

Catholic somebody who belongs to the Roman Catholic Church

chapel a small (often private) church

chaplain a man of God who works in a school, hospital or prison

churchyard the ground by a church where dead people are buried

cloak *(n)* a long, loose coat without sleeves

coach *(n)* a carriage pulled by horses

condemn to order a punishment for someone, e.g. condemning someone to death or to a number of years in prison

confess to say that you are guilty of doing something wrong

damp not dry; a little wet

devil a very bad or cruel person (or animal)

Devil (the) Satan, the enemy of God

eve the day or evening before an important day, e.g. Christmas Day

fingernail the hard part at the end of a finger

forfeit *(n)* something that a loser in a game must do, e.g. sing a song or tell a funny story

gentleman a polite word for a man

geology *(adj* **geological)** the study of rocks and stones

growl *(v)* to make a deep, rough sound like an angry dog

hanging judge a judge who often condemns people to be hanged

hanging shed a building where murderers were hanged with a
rope until they were dead

hide and seek a game in which people hide and other people look
for them

hunting chasing wild animals for food or fun

landlady a woman who rents rooms in a house or hotel for
money

landmark something easily seen from a distance (e.g. a tall tree or
rocks) that is helpful to travellers

landslide earth, rocks, etc. that slide down the side of a hill or
mountain

lantern a light in a glass and metal box, often used outside

lord a title for a nobleman (a rich and important man)

master *(n)* an old-fashioned word for a male employer

nervous afraid; worried

noose a small circle of rope that gets smaller when the other end
of the rope is pulled

oak a very hard, dark-coloured kind of wood

operator somebody who works a machine for connecting
telephone calls

pale *(adj)* with a light or weak colour

pliable easy to bend

poker a long metal tool for moving pieces of wood, etc., in a fire

pray to talk to God

rat a small animal with a long tail (like a mouse, but bigger and
fiercer)

rule *(n)* what you must, or must not do, in a game

servant someone who is paid to work in someone else's house

sober not having drunk any wine, beer, whisky, etc.

spirit the part of a person that is not the body; some people
believe the spirit lives after the body dies

squeak *(v)* to make a short, high sound

stag an adult male deer (a large animal with long horns)

stage *(n)* the platform in a theatre where the actors stand and move

stranger a person you do not know

strangle to kill someone by putting something round the neck and pulling it until the person cannot breathe

strike *(v)* to hit a bell to tell the hour, e.g. in a clock

style *(n)* an interesting and fashionable way of living

sweat *(n)* water that comes out of the skin when somebody is hot or frightened

swing *(v)* to move from side to side through the air

temple a building where people pray to a god

threaten to warn someone that you will punish or harm them if they do not do what you want

triumph *(n)* a great success

yard a piece of ground next to walls or buildings

Before Reading

1 **How much do you know about ghost stories? Choose the best words to complete this passage.**

You usually find ghosts in *old / new* buildings like *supermarkets / castles*, and they seem to prefer places that are *busy / deserted* and *brightly lit / rather dark*. They often appear *at night / during the day*, and they may arrive with a *cold / warm* wind. Ghosts are usually people who died *violently / peacefully*. They are mostly *cheerful / miserable*, they make people feel *uneasy / comfortable*, and they are often *dangerous / helpful* to the living. Meeting a ghost is, for most people, an *amusing / unpleasant* experience.

2 **Here are the titles of the stories. Can you guess which of the ghosts below you will find in each story?**

Smee / The Judge's House / The Stranger in the Mist / The Confession of Charles Linkworth / The Ghost Coach / Fullcircle

1 The ghost of a cruel person who takes pleasure in death
2 The ghost of someone who died in an accident during a game
3 The ghosts of people repeating the journey that took them to their deaths many years ago
4 A kind ghost who wants to help people, but instead puts them in danger
5 A ghost who wants to make people live calm, happy lives
6 The ghost of a murderer who wants to find peace

While Reading

Read the first story, *Smee*. Choose the best question-word for these questions, and then answer them.

Who / What

1 . . . didn't want to play hide and seek after dinner?
2 . . . is written on the pieces of paper in the game of 'Smee'?
3 . . . did Jack Sangston warn the players about?
4 . . . was sitting on the stairs two steps above Violet Sangston, between her and Captain Ransome?
5 . . . did Reggie touch in the clothes cupboard?
6 . . . did Tony Jackson bump into behind a curtain?
7 . . . did Mrs Gorman's finger-nails scratch?
8 . . . did Tony and Mrs Gorman dislike about the game?
9 . . . was Brenda Ford?

Read to the end of Chapter 6 in *The Judge's House*. Can you guess how the story will end? Choose one of these endings.

1 Moore survives his meeting with the judge, because the rats ring the alarm bell and Dr Thornhill arrives in time to rescue him.
2 Moore drives off the judge by throwing the old Bible at him, and then escapes from the house.
3 Moore dies of shock after his meeting with the judge.
4 The judge traps Moore and hangs him with the rope.
5 After a desperate fight between Moore and the judge, the house catches fire and Moore is burned to death.

Read *The Stranger in the Mist*. Here are some false sentences about it. Change them into true sentences.

1 Giles was pleased with Beverley's invitation because he was eager to study the old churches of Caernarvonshire.
2 In the mist, Giles took the wrong path because he had forgotten the landmarks he had noticed earlier.
3 Because the old man spoke in English, he was able to show Giles which path he should take.
4 If Giles had kept on following the path on the old man's map, he would have got home safely to Fablan Fawr.
5 The old man's map was out of date because the government had built a new road to Fablan Fawr.
6 The map that the old man had given Giles was almost the same as the map found in Mr Stevenson's pocket.
7 Madog ap Rhys always carried a copy of his map with him in case he lost his way in the mist.

Read *The Confession of Charles Linkworth*. Who said these words, and to whom? Who, or what, were they talking about?

1 'We can't find it anywhere.'
2 'Is it so very surprising if it remains in this world for a time?'
3 'There *was* something there.'
4 'Give it a chance to get to the telephone.'
5 'Will you send for the other gentleman?'
6 'He wants to tell you something. I think you can guess what it is.'
7 'I killed her. I confess. I want to be forgiven.'
8 'There is no rope, sir.'

Read *The Ghost Coach*. Then put these parts of sentences into the correct order, to make a paragraph of four sentences.

1 that he was travelling with three dead men.
2 He tried to make conversation with the three passengers, . . .
3 Later, he described his ghostly experience to the doctor, . . .
4 and their bloodless faces and burning eyes soon told Murray . . .
5 With a scream of horror he threw himself at the door, . . .
6 who refused to believe a word of it.
7 but they only stared at him without speaking, . . .
8 he noticed that the air smelt strangely damp and heavy.
9 but when the coach went over the edge of the steep drop, . . .
10 When Murray first got into the coach, . . .
11 Murray fell with it, down to the valley fifty feet below.

Read *Fullcircle*. For each sentence, circle B if it describes the Giffens at the beginning of the story, or E if it describes them at the end.

1 Julian drove a car. B/E
2 The Giffens organized classes and wrote books. B/E
3 Ursula was a Catholic, and Julian planned to become one. B/E
4 The Giffens used the chapel as a workroom. B/E
5 The Giffens wore ugly, unfashionable clothes. B/E
6 The Giffens drank wine. B/E
· 7 Julian rode a bike. B/E
8 Julian enjoyed fishing and shooting. B/E
9 The workroom was a chapel again. B/E
10 The Giffens had no style. B/E
11 Ursula's face was softer and prettier. B/E
12 The Giffens wore sensible clothes that suited them. B/E

After Reading

1 **What did Jack and Violet Sangston say while they waited for Tony and Mrs Gorman? Put this conversation in the right order and write in the speakers' names. Jack speaks first (number 2).**

1 _____ 'Mistake or not, it felt very strange. I think we should send Reggie to look for them.'

2 _____ 'This is getting silly. How much longer are we going to wait for Jackson and Mrs Gorman?'

3 _____ 'Of course they're all right! They're probably laughing in a corner somewhere. Very rude, I call it.'

4 _____ 'I don't care about that, as long as he finds them quickly.'

5 _____ 'I'm not so sure. I think there's something odd going on tonight – remember the thirteenth person on the stairs?'

6 _____ 'Yes, good idea. And he can tell them they've both got forfeits.'

7 _____ ' I think we've waited long enough. I'm getting rather worried, Jack. Do you think they're all right?'

8 _____ 'That was just a mistake. I must have counted somebody twice.'

2 **When he returned home that night, Dr Thornhill wrote his diary. Choose one suitable word to fill each gap.**

What an awful night _____ has been for Benchurch. _____ police have decided that _____ killed himself, but I _____ that very much; he _____ to me a perfectly _____ and cheerful young man, _____ at all the type _____ hang himself. But if _____ didn't do it, then

94

_____ did? Who made the _____ in the rope? Why _____ the rope
in two _____? The ends of the _____ had been bitten or _____, not
cut with a _____. Perhaps the rats did _____, though I can't
imagine _____. What also made me _____ was the judge's face
_____ that picture. I have _____ seen such a cruel, _____ face. And
he seemed _____ be staring at that _____ boy with a triumphant
_____. People say he was _____ hard man, a real _____ judge, who
showed no _____ to anyone. It's a _____ idea, but I can't _____
thinking that perhaps his _____ wanted one last hanging . . .

3 In *The Stranger in the Mist*, if Giles and Madog had spoken the same
   language, they might have had a conversation like this. Complete
   their conversation. (Use as many words as you like.)

   GILES: Oh, I'm so glad to see you. Can you help me? I'm lost.
   MADOG: Hello, young man. Where _____?
   GILES: Fablan Fawr. Do you know it?
   MADOG: Yes indeed. I've _____ and I know _____.
   GILES: You must do, if you can walk around in this mist. Do you
          come across many people in these hills?
   MADOG: Whenever there's a mist, I come out and _____.
          That's why I _____. Look, _____.
   GILES: Ah, a map. Yes, I see. And this is the path I should take?
   MADOG: Yes, that _____. But please _____.
   GILES: No, no, I mustn't take your map.
   MADOG: But I _____. In fact, a few years ago I _____.
   GILES: Really? Right here, you say? And was he lost too?
   MADOG: Yes, but I _____, and I'm sure he _____.
   GILES: Well, I'll follow in his footsteps, then. That's very kind of
          you, and thank you very much for your help.

4 Put these sentences in order, to make a summary of the chaplain's story in *The Confession of Charles Linkworth*.

1 Then the doctor's telephone rang . . .
2 When the phone rang again, . . .
3 who told me that Linkworth had telephoned him, . . .
4 and a few minutes later we saw him in the room with us, . . .
5 Two days after Linkworth died, . . .
6 so I spoke the words of forgiveness to him.
7 and a soft voice asked me to forgive him.
8 I had dinner with Dr Teesdale, . . .
9 I asked for a sign from the dead man . . .
10 asking to speak to me.
11 Linkworth confessed to his crime . . .
12 which was a most horrible experience.

5 In *The Ghost Coach* there are a number of questions that are not answered. What do *you* think are the answers to these questions?

1 When the bell rings, just after Murray arrives at the house, why does Jacob say to him 'That's for you', when his master does not even know that Murray has entered the house?
2 Why does the old man give Murray a good meal, but eat only bread and milk himself?
3 Why did the old man smile for the first time after giving Murray directions to the coach? Did he deliberately send Murray to ride in the ghost coach? If so, why do you think he did this?
4 Jacob told Murray that four passengers had been killed in the accident, but when Murray got into the ghost coach, there were only three passengers inside. Why was that, do you think?

6 Write an advertisement for the house called 'Fullcircle'. Use these notes to help you.

- Situated in ...
- Near to house – wall, lake, wood, rose garden
- Designed by ...
- First owner Lord Carteron, who ...
- Interesting parts of house: walls, windows, staircase, chapel, library ...
- Would suit owners who ...

7 Imagine that these stories appear in the newspapers. Which of these headlines go with which stories? Which ones do you prefer? Why?

MURDERER CONFESSES – AFTER DEATH

THIRTEENTH GUEST AT CHRISTMAS PARTY IS GHOST

'GHOST HOUSE HAS CHANGED MY FRIENDS,' SAYS DR SWOPE

LOST MAN'S RIDE IN COACH OF TERROR

THREE STEPS FROM CLIFF EDGE – VISITOR'S LUCKY ESCAPE

'MY RIDE WITH DEAD MEN' – INJURED TRAVELLER SPEAKS

MYSTERY DEATH OF STUDENT IN LOCAL HOUSE

CHAPLAIN'S CALL FROM UNHAPPY SPIRIT

DEAD WOMAN APPEARS IN PARTY GAME

THE MAGIC OF A HOUSE – 'I'M A CHANGED MAN,' SAYS OWNER

GHOST OF MADOG AP RHYS NEARLY KILLS VISITOR

ALARM BELL RINGS AS STUDENT DIES

8 Which story did you find most interesting? Which was most unusual, and which was most frightening? Why?

9 Perhaps this is what some of the characters in the stories were thinking. Which six characters were they (one from each story), and what was happening in the story at that moment?

1 It's strange that it should be such a bright and pleasant morning when a man is going to his death. I do wish he would confess. I'm sure he would feel more at peace if he did. But I have tried, and he refuses to change.

2 I'm so glad that Harry was able to see the house. I knew he would find it as delightful as I do, even with its silly new owners. They're good, kind people, of course, but thank goodness we got away without meeting their awful friends.

3 Poor boy! How he jumped when he touched my hand in the clothes cupboard! Who, I wonder, will find me in this new hiding-place? Someone is sure to slip behind the curtains and put out their hand . . .

4 I don't like this at all. Our guest should have been back hours ago. It's terrible when it's misty like this. It's just like the time a few years ago when that other poor young man . . . I'll try shouting once again – perhaps he'll hear me this time . . .

5 There goes our visitor. I hope he's careful – it's a steep drop where the wall is broken. Will the coach come? I think the old man imagines it, myself. But strange things happen in lonely places . . .

6 What . . . what's happening? What's that noise? Oh, my God – it's the alarm bell. I knew something would happen. That poor young man. I must go to the house at once – I just hope it won't be too late . . .

ABOUT THE AUTHORS

E. F. BENSON
Edward Frederic Benson was born in 1867 to a distinguished English family; his father was to become Archbishop of Canterbury. He first worked as an archaeologist, and later became a full-time writer. He is best known for his 'Lucia' stories, which give an amusing view of English village life, full of jealousy, plots, whispers and gossip. These stories were later very popular as a television series. Benson was also successful in a very different area – ghost and horror stories. He wrote a great number of these, and preferred to have horrible creatures as their subjects rather than people. He died in 1940.

JOHN BUCHAN
Buchan was born in Scotland in 1875. He became a lawyer, then a Member of Parliament in 1927. In 1935 he was given the title of Baron Tweedsmuir and became Governor-General of Canada, a position he held until he died in 1940. He wrote more than fifty books, and is most famous for his adventure stories, like *The Thirty-Nine Steps* (retold in Bookworms at Stage 4). His other works include books about real people, such as Sir Walter Scott and Oliver Cromwell, and short stories.

A. M. BURRAGE
Alfred McLellan Burrage (1889–1956) was a well-known English novelist. He also enjoyed writing about ghosts and horror, and produced two novels and many short stories in this genre. 'Smee' comes from his collection entitled *Someone in the Room*.

AMELIA B. EDWARDS

Amelia Edwards was born in England in 1831, and died in 1892. She sold her first poem at the age of seven, and the first of her eight novels was published in 1855. She regularly wrote stories for magazines edited by Charles Dickens, often writing the ghost story for the Christmas issue. In her forties she became interested in ancient history, and travelled to Egypt; she wrote many books about Egypt in later life.

A. N. L. MUNBY

Alan Noel Latimer Munby was born in England in 1913 and died in 1974. The son of an architect, he studied history, then trained as a librarian, later becoming librarian at King's College, Cambridge, where he had studied. Munby was inspired by the writer M. R. James, who was famous for his ghost stories (some are retold in Bookworms, in *The Unquiet Grave* at Stage 4). Munby wrote all his ghost stories between 1943 and 1945, while he was a prisoner of war in Eichstätt camp in Germany.

BRAM STOKER

Stoker (1847–1912) has been called 'one of the least-known authors of one of the best-known books'. As a child, he enjoyed listening to and writing ghost stories, and predicted that one day his writing would make him famous. He worked as a lawyer, editor, and theatre manager, and wrote novels, short stories and non-fiction. His most famous work is *Dracula*, which has appeared in six film versions, on television, as a play, and as a comic. *Dracula* (retold in Bookworms at Stage 2) has never been out of print since it was published in 1899.

ABOUT BOOKWORMS

OXFORD BOOKWORMS LIBRARY
Classics • True Stories • Fantasy & Horror • Human Interest
Crime & Mystery • Thriller & Adventure

The OXFORD BOOKWORMS LIBRARY offers a wide range of original and adapted stories, both classic and modern, which take learners from elementary to advanced level through six carefully graded language stages:

Stage 1 (400 headwords)	**Stage 4** (1400 headwords)
Stage 2 (700 headwords)	**Stage 5** (1800 headwords)
Stage 3 (1000 headwords)	**Stage 6** (2500 headwords)

More than fifty titles are also available on cassette, and there are many titles at Stages 1 to 4 which are specially recommended for younger learners. In addition to the introductions and activities in each Bookworm, resource material includes photocopiable test worksheets and Teacher's Handbooks, which contain advice on running a class library and using cassettes, and the answers for the activities in the books.

———————————

Several other series are linked to the OXFORD BOOKWORMS LIBRARY. They range from highly illustrated readers for young learners, to playscripts, non-fiction readers, and unsimplified texts for advanced learners.

Oxford Bookworms Starters   *Oxford Bookworms Factfiles*
Oxford Bookworms Playscripts   *Oxford Bookworms Collection*

Details of these series and a full list of all titles in the OXFORD BOOKWORMS LIBRARY can be found in the *Oxford English* catalogues. A selection of titles from the OXFORD BOOKWORMS LIBRARY can be found on the next pages.

Do Androids Dream of Electric Sheep?

PHILIP K. DICK

Retold by Andy Hopkins and Joc Potter

San Francisco lies under a cloud of radioactive dust. People live in half-deserted apartment buildings, and keep electric animals as pets because so many real animals have died. Most people emigrate to Mars – unless they have a job to do on Earth.

Like Rick Deckard – android killer for the police and owner of an electric sheep. This week he has to find, identify, and kill six androids which have escaped from Mars. They're machines, but they look and sound and think like humans – clever, dangerous humans. They will be hard to kill.

The film *Bladerunner* was based on this famous novel.

I, Robot

ISAAC ASIMOV

Retold by Rowena Akinyemi

A human being is a soft, weak creature. It needs constant supplies of air, water, and food; it has to spend a third of its life asleep, and it can't work if the temperature is too hot or too cold.

But a robot is made of strong metal. It uses electrical energy directly, never sleeps, and can work in any temperature. It is stronger, more efficient – and sometimes more human than human beings.

Isaac Asimov was one of the greatest science-fiction writers, and these short stories give us an unforgettable and terrifying vision of the future.

BOOKWORMS · CLASSICS · STAGE 5

Wuthering Heights

EMILY BRONTË

Retold by Clare West

The wind is strong on the Yorkshire moors. There are few trees, and fewer houses, to block its path. There is one house, however, that does not hide from the wind. It stands out from the hill and challenges the wind to do its worst. The house is called Wuthering Heights.

When Mr Earnshaw brings a strange, small, dark child back home to Wuthering Heights, it seems he has opened his doors to trouble. He has invited in something that, like the wind, is safer kept out of the house.

BOOKWORMS · THRILLER & ADVENTURE · STAGE 5

Brat Farrar

JOSEPHINE TEY

Retold by Ralph Mowat

'You look exactly like him! You can take the dead boy's place and no one will ever know the difference. You'll be rich for life!'

And so the plan was born. At first Brat Farrar fought against the idea; it was criminal, it was dangerous. But in the end he was persuaded, and a few weeks later Patrick Ashby came back from the dead and went home to inherit the family house and fortune. The Ashby family seemed happy to welcome Patrick home, but Brat soon realized that somewhere there was a time-bomb ticking away, waiting to explode . . .

BOOKWORMS • CRIME & MYSTERY • STAGE 5

King's Ransom

ED McBAIN

Retold by Rosalie Kerr

'Calling all cars, calling all cars. Here's the story on the Smoke Rise kidnapping. The missing boy is eight years old, fair hair, wearing a red sweater. His name is Jeffry Reynolds, son of Charles Reynolds, chauffeur to Douglas King.'

The police at the 87th Precinct hate kidnappers. And these kidnappers are stupid, too. They took the wrong boy – the chauffeur's son instead of the son of the rich tycoon, Douglas King. And they want a ransom of $500,000.

A lot of money. But it's not too much to pay for a little boy's life . . . is it?

BOOKWORMS • FANTASY & HORROR • STAGE 6

Meteor and Other Stories

JOHN WYNDHAM

Retold by Patrick Nobes

It was just a smooth round metal ball, less than a metre in diameter. Although it was still hot from its journey through the huge nothingness of space, it looked quite harmless. But what was it, exactly? A meteor, perhaps – just one of those pieces of rock from outer space that occasionally fall down on to the planet Earth. But meteors don't usually make strange hissing sounds . . .

In this collection of four of his famous science-fiction stories, John Wyndham creates visions of the future that make us think carefully about the way we live now.